6 pairs of sandals

*Yesterday's Footsteps
and Today's Women's Ministry*

By Dr. Deborah Waterbury

TABLE *of* CONTENTS

Introduction

I think it is fairly safe to say that all of us as Christian women desire for the church to grow and succeed in its mission. Of course we want that! However, I also think it's fairly safe to say that the majority of mainstream Christians are quite happy to let the "called" carry out that mission or the "ministers" be responsible for its success. Unfortunately, the complacency so prevalent in many of our churches is due to the complacency of its individual members, and we women are no exception.

Churches are floundering, especially here in America, though I travel all over the world and I've seen the same issues elsewhere. Of course, there are many very large churches, but numbers aren't really the issue, are they? The issue is the Great Commission. The issue is fulfilling our one true mission on this earth from a starting point of loneliness, isolation, and despair. The issue is that churches could be filled to the brim, even having to add more chairs, but they are floundering within, therefore also floundering without. And since my calling and my heart are for women, this is where I see the need so apparent.

Women are desperate for ministry, for fellowship, and for relationship.

Women, though of course ministered to by the men in the church, can only really and truly be ministered to by other women. Women communicate in their own language – in "woman speak" if you will – while men speak in a vernacular that only they understand. There's nothing wrong with that. We're different. God created us to be different, and each gender is to shine to our Father's glory through those differences. The problem arises when the only way in which women in the local church are being ministered to is by the men in the church. A gaping hole exists – a way of communicating God's glorious truths is absent – when women hear only from men. Consequently, a void exists in the very areas in which women are craving help: in ministry, in fellowship, and in relationship.

Let me clarify. What breaks my heart as I travel around the world speaking and ministering to women in their local churches is walking away from those ladies when the conference or retreat has ended. It saddens me to know that nothing is in place within their church community that might allow women to share and delight in the truths of who they are, both as the bride of Christ and as women of God. When I board the plane and head back home, I generally leave behind a group of women on fire and hungry for more of what they've just heard and shared with one another within the confines of the conference or retreat. These same women walk right back into that same vacant ministry hole from which they were attempting to find a way out. They want to move forward. They want to share what they've learned. They want to continue within their own church family the beautiful camaraderie they have just experienced together as women of God, but nothing is in place for women to minister to women, and no one really knows where to start to alleviate that problem.

Ladies, one of the truths associated with being a Christian, whether man or woman, is that we are all called to ministry, and as members of a local church body, there is a special call for us to minister to each other within that church. Each of us must find the place where we fit best and then actively minister to one another in our home churches. Women must minister to other women in ways that only they can, while men should do the same in ministering to men.

However, the problem is that most of us don't know where to start, do we? And most of us, even if we did have an inkling of where to start, feel completely inadequate to do so. When older women are asked to mentor younger women, just as Paul recommended to Titus (Titus 2:3), the older women say, "I don't feel adequate." When younger women are asked to lead small groups or even speak one-on-one to another woman, they say, "I don't know enough." And the result is that we return to our churches and our homes after a conference or retreat, full of knowledge of our Lord and Savior, but with little or no outlet for such knowledge.

Consequently, the church will suffer, the church members will suffer, and the Great Commission will suffer.

So, what do we do about it? That's where this book comes in and, prayerfully, where revival begins. It's time for each of us to shed the dark cloak of inadequacy and don the glorious garment of discipleship and mission. All of us are called to it, and all of us can do it. What I want to do in the next few pages is simply to give you some areas where women ministering to women can occur within our local churches and, with God's help, to open your eyes to places where you might step in and begin ministering.

God has promised that He will do a "new thing" in His church (Isaiah 43:18-19), but there are contingencies on our both seeing this new thing and then taking part in it. Most people are content to watch the new thing happen, which is okay. However, some get to have the amazing blessing of actually doing the new thing, of actually fulfilling the call that is on all of us as believers in Christ as our Savior and our eternal Bridegroom.

Will you step out and do a new thing, or will you be content in simply watching others do it? Will you join the ranks of the men and women of God written about in the Bible who boldly and unabashedly shed the garment of doubt and reticence in exchange for the one that shines like the beacon that all believers are supposed to be in this lost world?

In the next few chapters, I'm going to give you six specific areas of need for women to minister to and disciple other women within every local church. Along with each of these areas, I'm going to show you six women in the Bible who fulfilled that place within the body of believers and then explain how each of those women exemplified a woman who boldly stepped out and fulfilled this role. Each of these biblical women literally stepped out in her beautiful sandals, showing us how every single woman can fulfill her particular role in ministering to women in her home church.

This kind of purpose and place in the church won't be sought by everyone, but for those who do, God will move victoriously, both in their lives and in His kingdom work, to perform all to His glory and majesty. Come on; take a chance. You can do this. God will not let you fail. After all, it's He who does the work, right?

The New Thing

"Remember not the former things, nor consider the things of old. Behold, I am doing a new thing; now it springs forth, do you not perceive it? I will make a way in the wilderness and rivers in the desert." – Isaiah 43:18, 19

This beautiful passage is a tremendous promise, not only to the Jews to whom Isaiah was writing, but also to us as we attempt to move forward without dwelling on the past. However, lest we take passages of Scripture out of context, let's take a few minutes to examine the time frame in which Isaiah is writing these verses. Let's look at exactly what he was prophesying to the Israelites and to what he is calling them as he wrote about this new thing. From there we can safely move into its application for us today as God also calls us to look upon Him as He does a new thing in our lives. From there may we find the courage to step forward in our own sandals and find our place in the ministry of women to women in the church.

THE CONTEXT

Isaiah prophesied to the children of Israel between 739-685 BC. Isaiah died in 680 BC, but in chapter 43 of his book, he prophesied that the Babylonian kingdom would fall, ending the Israelite captivity. Keep in mind that the Babylonian empire would not take over Judah until 605 BC, some 75 years after Isaiah's death, so this prophecy about their downfall before they had even taken over was astounding. At the very least, it must have been astounding to his contemporary listeners. The Babylonians did fall, in fact, at the hands of the Persian king, Cyrus, in 586 BC, which was 144 years after Isaiah died, thereby fulfilling what the prophet had foretold in chapter 43.

It is also important to understand the immediate situation of the people to whom Isaiah was prophesying. It was a tremendously bleak period for the Israelite nation. They were in captivity, and it seemed that none of the promises of this new land and the blessings of being God's chosen people would come to fruition. They had lived through many years of Egyptian tyranny, reduced to living as slaves before Moses led them out to seek the Promised Land. One would think that the miracles performed by our Lord on their behalf were great enough to be remembered and to produce faith in His promises, but the Israelites were human, after all. What is universally true of all human memory is that it is short. We tend to forget how faithful God has been in the past when we look at our present circumstances. The Israelites were having a hard time remembering the freedom brought by God and instead were in despair over circumstances that simply kept repeating themselves.

That's understandable. We do the same thing all of the time. We forget. And just like us, even though God had never wavered in his faithfulness to them, they were continuously unfaithful to Him. They rebelled, followed after other gods, refused to keep the Law, and then found themselves repeatedly facing exactly the same situations, even after Isaiah had spoken to them.

Do you ever wonder why we often tend to find ourselves licking the same wounds and asking for forgiveness from the same sins over and over again? Isn't it a wonderful thing that our God is, by His very nature, the epitome of faithfulness and that His character will never return our lack of faithfulness in like kind?

The Israelites had many victories in their past. Not only had they been delivered out of Egyptian bondage, but they had also been victorious in the land of Canaan over many prospective conquerors who sought to take from them the Promised Land, and they had survived a split in their country. They had much to remember, but now they were in bondage again, and they were having a hard time recalling all that the Lord had done for them.

What's so very interesting about Isaiah's prophecy, as we see it in this chapter, particularly in verses eighteen and nineteen, is that the prophet doesn't tell the Israelites to hold fast to God's faithfulness simply because of what God had accomplished in the past, though that certainly should have been enough. No, God knows us better than we know ourselves, and though the constancy of His character, as manifested in their past, should have been enough, God in His mercy gave them more. He always gives us more.

Isaiah 43:18 and 19 say, *"Remember not the former things, nor consider the things of old. Behold, I am doing a new thing."* In essence, God was not telling his children to forget everything He'd done in the past, but simply that they shouldn't dwell there. Instead, He was telling them that what He'd done in the past for them, though miraculous and genuinely amazing, could not be compared to what He had for them in the future. He was saying, "Hold on, my children! What I've done for you before is nothing compared to what I'm going to do! It will be new and wonderful and better than you can ever imagine!"

> John Calvin wrote:
> "This (Isaiah's prophesy) shows more clearly what the Prophet meant in the preceding verse, for he declares that there shall be 'a new work,' that is, a work unheard of and uncommon, and which, on account of its greatness and excellence, shall throw into the shade the reputation of all other works; in the same manner as the brightness of the sun, when it fills heaven and earth, causes the stars to disappear. "[1]

What an amazing promise to receive from the Lord of the universe, especially in light of their past failures! The Israelites had recompensed God's gift of the temple with idol worship. They had substituted God's truths with proclaiming and living lies. They had responded to God's commandments by living as if they were merely suggestions. They had repaid God's gift of wealth and prosperity by exploiting the poor. They had been given God, and they returned that tremendous gift with rebellion.

But God was saying not only that they shouldn't dwell on just His past faithfulness, but also that they shouldn't dwell on their past failures. God's grace and mercy extend so far beyond our inadequacies that even when we don't deserve His promises, He gives them to us anyway. God wasn't holding the Israelites' past sins against them, and He wasn't withholding His wonderful future for them because of those sins either.

---

[1] Calvin, John, Commentary on Isaiah, Vol. 3, The Bible Truth Forum, www.bibletruthforum.com

Just as God instructed the Israelites, He is calling us not to dwell on the past, but to live in Him for His glorious promises for our future. Isaiah 55:7 says, *"Let the wicked forsake his way, and the unrighteous man his thoughts; let him return to the Lord, that he may have compassion on him, and to our God, for he will abundantly pardon."*

In the short term, God was promising His people that their deliverance from Egypt was nothing compared to the way He would deliver them from the Babylonians. However, in the longer and more important term, God was promising them final deliverance through Jesus Christ, bringing them perfectly and completely into His presence for all eternity. Nothing they had done would disrupt the future He had planned for them. Jeremiah 29:11 reminds us, "For I know the plans I have for you, declares the LORD, plans for welfare and not for evil, to give you a future and a hope."

What God does is and always will be determined by Himself, by His character of mercy and grace, and will always work to His glory. Never has God been ruled or steered by humanity, though His love for humanity has never altered. What God was promising the Israelites through Isaiah was profound, not simply because surpassing what He had already done was going to be astounding, but also because His plans for His people are determined by His glory, which is ultimately for their good. *"And we know that for those who love God all things work together for good, for those who are called according to his purpose."* (Romans 8:28)

And finally, God's promise carried a sense of immediacy, even as He proclaimed His sovereignty: *"Behold, I am doing a new thing; now it springs forth, do you not perceive it? I will make a way in the wilderness and rivers in the desert."* (Isaiah 43:19)

Even though we must keep in mind that a thousand years is like one day to our Father (2 Peter 3:8), He wants us to hang onto His promises for our lives with this same sense of immediacy.

17

Through Isaiah, God was promising the Israelites that even though they might not see it in their limited vision, He was already about the business of bringing His promises to pass. Our circumstances will sometimes keep us from seeing the beauty of God's plan, but in faith we must remember that if He says something, He will do it. Indeed, He is already doing it! He's moving in the hearts and minds of others, putting peoples and places in order so that when the time comes, His promise for us will come to light.

And notice that it is certainly He who will do it. God is in the business of making ways in the wilderness and running rivers through the deserts of our lives. He promises, He works it out, and He paves the way. His plans for Israel would not be thwarted, and ultimately His promise was fulfilled for all of God's people in Jesus Christ, His Son and our Savior.

THE APPLICATION

You might be asking yourself now what any of this has to do with women ministering to women in our local churches. If you remember earlier when I wrote about this beautiful call on all of our lives to move and work in the lives of one another, then you'll also remember that I used the phrase "new thing." Indeed, God is calling all of us to a new thing, to forget our past inadequacies and failures and to instead embrace what He has called us to do. Just as He spoke through the prophet Isaiah to the nation of Israel, telling them to forget their past in light of His great promise for their future, He is speaking that message to each of us.

However, forgetting past failures and embracing future opportunities requires a great deal of introspection and even more faith. You see, God is definitely calling all of us to service to each other and, I believe, particularly within the confines of the local church body. He is definitely calling each of us to get out of our comfort zones and fulfill His unique call on our lives to spread the Gospel to every living creature, but before we can ever be successful in that call, we have to minister to each other, and we have to start with our own church family.

For women, that has to start with ministry to each other, which consequently has to start with believing this promise is also for you. When God told the Israelites, "Behold, I am doing a new thing," He meant for all of us to see that "thing" in regards to our lives in the here and now. The new thing may be only new to you, if you haven't moved in it yet, but it is new nonetheless. And God is saying, "Forget the past. Look at me. Trust me. I am going to do a new thing in your church and in the women I have put in your path. Can you see it? Will you trust me?" This interpretation doesn't discount the truth that the ultimate new thing God did was in Jesus, but the new thing for us practically in His kingdom must also be ensured so that the promises in Jesus are truly "Yes and Amen!" (2 Corinthians 1:20).

The truth is that few will do this new thing, though all are called to it. It's hard to step out in faith this way. It's extremely difficult to look past your past and forge ahead in ministry. Do you know why? Because when you do, your purpose in life will no longer be about you. It will no longer be about your inadequacies or your circumstances or your anything. Now it will be about others, about their hearts and their needs and their pain. Now it will be about God, about His purposes, His mission, and His glory.

Consequently, 95% of Christian women will be content to follow someone else who is doing the new thing, and that's okay. Following the new thing certainly won't discount their salvation or God's love for them. However, for those few who are willing to step into the sandals of those who have gone before us, stepping out in faith and doing the new thing, there are blessings innumerable and joy incomparable in store for them. Pain, heartache, and trials will come, but they will pale in comparison to the former. God has chosen each of us to be instruments of His grace. What better way to manifest this call than to minister to the women in your immediate Christian family.

Within the contents of this book, six places are identified where you can fulfill this call in your church, and six pairs of sandals have shown us the way. Not every church is the same. Demographics are different, locations are different, and needs are different. However, these six areas are broad enough, I think, that every single woman can insert herself into one of them, depending on her individual strengths and/or the immediate needs of her church.

Along with each of these areas will be a study of a specific woman from the Bible who fulfilled the aspects of that area during her lifetime, walking a path that we can follow ourselves. God put each of these women in his Word on purpose, and one of the lessons I think they teach us is how to minister to one another as women of God. The six pairs of sandals we will be covering belong to the following women, along with the specific ministry these sandals walked within:

Women's Ministry Leader ⎯ Deborah
Small Group Leader ⎯ Lydia
Mentor ⎯ Elizabeth
Servant Disciple ⎯ Dorcas
Prayer Warrior ⎯ Hannah
Teacher ⎯ Priscilla

These examples are not mutually exclusive, nor are they meant to be all inclusive. In each category, other Bible women could have been used as examples, and Christian ladies today might also fulfill God's call in multiple ways. However, these examples are meant to be an encouragement to each of you, no matter what your particular gifts are, so that the necessity and importance of all ministry between women is seen as vital within God's church. Consequently, nuances within these areas of ministry exist that I didn't specifically name.

For example, you may feel a desire to minister to new believers in your church. Whereas that is a specific call, it might also fit within the confines of small group leader, mentorship, or even one-to-one ministry. My desire was to be as general as I could while including every potential area of ministry so that no one would be left out.

I cannot stress strongly enough that ministering to women is not a particular call. This is not for an elect set of women who have some great strength or a knack for speaking or a penchant for entertaining. This call is a general call to all women within the church, but what is true of all calls within God's kingdom is also true here. Many are called, but few answer. Unlike other calls, however, as in the call to teach or the call to a foreign mission field, this call is unlimited in its scope. It includes every woman who considers herself a child of God and the bride of her Bridegroom. Still, I realize that few will answer it.

Will you? Will you step out of your comfort zone, away from the actual loneliness within that zone, in order to examine the area of ministry that is the perfect fit for you? Will you step into one of these six pairs of sandals? Because one of these pairs of shoes is yours. You need only determine which one.

If only a few women in every church would answer this absolutely general call, I'm convinced that there would be revival. If we don't start with revival in our own hearts and let that spread to our church home, how can we expect any kind of revival outside of its four walls?

As you read, my prayer for each of you echoes Paul's prayer for the Philippian church, *"And it is my prayer that your love may abound more and more, with knowledge and all discernment, so that you may approve what is excellent, and so be pure and blameless for the day of Christ, filled with the fruit of righteousness that comes through Jesus Christ, to the glory and praise of God."* (Philippians 1:9-11)

Deborah

and the Women's Ministry Leader

... 2

In the area of ministry by women to women in their local churches, I thought it might be best to address the women's ministry leader first for a couple of reasons. First, this is the area that most people think of when they think about women's ministry. In the last forty or fifty years, there has been a trend in contemporary churches toward having a leader for specific ministries within the local church. This is a relatively new concept, since up until the mid-1900's the only leaders in the church were strictly pastoral, i.e. teachers, elders, pastors, etc. Then as churches became much more mainstream, the concept of leaders for specialized groups within the church was born. Consequently, many churches began creating positions for children's ministry leaders, youth ministry leaders, singles' ministry leaders, men's ministry leaders, women's ministry leaders, and so on.

Because this idea was born into the "leadership" family of roles within the church, it also became much more segregated as to who would take on such a role. Women's ministry leaders were viewed as women with specialized gifts of leadership, teaching, organization, and even pastoral skills. The result has been two-fold: fewer women felt qualified to lead in a women's ministry, and the lines between pastoral care and leadership organization have become blurred. As a result, many churches are moving away from having such specialized leadership roles within the church, and the consequence of that has been that either women are left with nothing, or they are forced to look outside of their local church family for women-to-women ministry.

My second reason for discussing this area of ministry first is somewhat linked to the problem stated just now. The view that women who take on the position of women's ministry leader must have a certain skill set has caused many women to feel that they can't do it because they can't teach or they can't be a "pastor." Truth be told, the gifts needed to lead a women's ministry in one's local church aren't necessarily what one might expect, especially given the recent history of these roles as they have played themselves out. Actually, if done correctly, the only effective strategies of a good women's ministry leader are those that uplift and encourage the women in her church while supporting the pastoral team, undergirding their leadership by her own. No special gifts are necessary to take on such a role. The only thing needed is a heart bent toward God's Word while serving women.

Now, that's not to say that a teaching gift isn't useful for one serving as a leader of women's ministry, but it absolutely isn't vital. At the end of the day, it's about service, which, as you will see, really is the common denominator for all six areas discussed in this book.

For the area of women's ministry leader, I've decided to use Deborah from Judges 4-5 as our example. Please know that I did not do so because she was so influential or even because she was a prophetess and judge in Israel. Instead, the unique and beautiful aspects of Deborah's character enabled her to lead, and these characteristics precisely should encompass any woman who believes that this is the area in which God is leading her to serve.

YESTERDAY'S FOOTSTEPS

DEBORAH ⁓ a Humble and Courageous Leader

The history of Deborah is contained within Judges 4-5, and we can read in the very first verse of chapter 4 exactly what the atmosphere was in Israel at this time: *"And the people of Israel again did what was evil in the sight of the LORD after Ehud died."*

During the time of the judges in Israel, a seemingly endless cycle took place, where the Lord would send an enemy to come in as judgment against the people's evil deeds, the people would cry out for deliverance in their distress, and God would send a deliverer, generally in the form of a judge, to rescue them. Deborah was one of these twelve judges, and in her we see the characteristics of humility, strength, and leadership that exemplify a faithful woman of God.

From the time of Joshua, the Israelites had continually rebelled against God and His ordinances, and what resulted was a non-stop surge of their enemies re-grouping in an attempt to reclaim the land. During the term of Deborah's time as judge, the king of Canaan, Jabin, saw an opportunity for attack, and because of his expert use of chariots, the people greatly feared what he might do. They were afraid and once again cried out to the Lord to deliver them.

Interestingly, they cried out to Deborah for deliverance because even the Levitical priests, who were charged with leading the people in piety and purity, had become so corrupt that they were untrustworthy, even to a people who were in full rebellion. This reaction of the people was undoubtedly a strong rebuke from God against his anointed priests, for not only were the people crying out for another judge to save them, but they were also crying out for a woman to save them. It is in this atmosphere that we see the unquestionable attributes of this woman leader.

1. Deborah — *the Humble Woman*

First, it is paramount that we point out that Deborah, though a prophetess and judge, didn't presume a leadership role. The Bible tells us in Judges 4:5, *"She* [Deborah] *used to sit under the palm of Deborah between Ramah and Bethel in the hill country of Ephraim, and the people of Israel came up to her for judgment."*

Deborah very easily could have taken up the mantle of leadership over the people, but she obviously knew God's law and respected her role within it. Without question, she was a prophet, and inasmuch as this was so, she was vitally important to God's people. God made no distinction between the genders when it came to those who would hear His voice. Men and women alike were given this gift, and both were equally important. However, Deborah understood that her role in God's kingdom didn't diminish her importance in it. In humility, she accepted a leadership role in God's work while refusing to assume a position that would have usurped God's design.

2. Deborah — *the Humble Spokesperson*

In this humility, another characteristic of Deborah that qualified her for leadership is that she spoke only what God said. When she called for Barak, the son of Abinoam, to talk to him about his leadership militarily, she didn't offer up her own ideas or opinions. Judges 4:6 records her as saying, *"Has not the LORD, the God of Israel, commanded you...?"*

Again, her position within Israel, along with the obvious respect she had from the people, might have given way to pride in her own words. She might have given Barak a piece of her mind, berating him for his lack of leadership. But she didn't. She simply spoke to him what God had said and then supported him in his leadership. Deborah knew the beauty of God's perfect Word, and she saw no need to insert any of herself into the situation, even though she very easily could have.

3. Deborah — *the Courageous Leader*

Deborah was a very courageous woman. Given the social mores of that time period, it was courageous enough for her to prophesy in the name of the Lord. Although the Bible doesn't record certain specifics, it's probably safe to assume that some people weren't completely happy with a woman holding this kind of position. Deborah not only stepped out courageously when called by God to prophesy to His people, but she audaciously met with the man who should have been leading, gave him solid counsel, and then even went into battle with him, supporting him with her very presence. Judges 4:8-10 says, *"Barak said to her, 'If you will go with me, I will go, but if you will not go with me, I will not go.' And she said, 'I will surely go with you....' And Barak called out Zebulun and Naphtali to Kedesh. And 10,000 men went up at his heels, and Deborah went up with him."*

4. Deborah — *the Singer of God's Glory*

When the victory was secured and Israel was delivered out of the hands of Jabin, king of Canaan, Judges 5 records the song sung by Deborah and Barak, and in this song we see Deborah's next characteristic that qualified her for leadership. She gave God all of the glory for the victory. Judges 5:3-5 records her singing,

> *"Hear, O kings; give ear, O princes;*
> *to the LORD I will sing;*
> *I will make melody to the LORD, the God of Israel.*
>
> *LORD, when you went out from Seir,*
> *when you marched from the region of Edom,*
> *the earth trembled*
> *and the heavens dropped,*
> *yes, the clouds dropped water.*
> *The mountains quaked before the LORD,*
> *even Sinai before the LORD, the God of Israel."*

Once again, humility in leadership qualifies some to lead and not others. Deborah could have very easily sung of her own qualities. She obviously was very wise and very influential. Undoubtedly, her advice to Barak helped him in military conquest, and even her presence seemed to soothe him as he went to battle. It would have been so very easy for her to take credit, even a little, for this great victory that subsequently brought peace to the nation of Israel for forty years afterward. But she didn't. Deborah knew that only God deserves the glory, and only He should receive it.

5. Deborah ⁓ *the "Mother of Israel"*

Finally, Deborah embraced her role as "mother of Israel." During her song in Judges 5:7, she sang, *"The villagers ceased in Israel; they ceased to be until I arose; I, Deborah, arose as a mother in Israel."*

Once again, it might have been very easy for her to call herself something more. After all, "mother" was not a designation in that time period that brought the kind of notoriety and respect that other titles might have. A mother was still a woman. However, Deborah humbly embraced her role in Israel, caring not for the title or the respect of man. Her one and only concern was for the advancement of God's people and ultimately of his Word, which definitely made her a likely candidate for stepping into a new thing in God's kingdom.

TODAY'S FOOTSTEPS

A Humble and Courageous Women's Minister

What are we to take away from what this great woman of faith teaches us? How does what the Bible says about Deborah guide those who feel led to take up this particular mantle of leadership within their local churches? Truly Deborah led with faith and dignity, and those two qualities alone are reason enough for her to be discussed in two important chapters in the history of God's people. However, if you are contemplating walking in the sandals of Deborah and leading the women in your church, or even if that is currently your position, the qualities outlined about the way in which

Deborah led are the ones most necessary in women's ministry leadership, and they are the ones that bear attention and application.

1. She has Security as a Woman

First, women who minister to women, especially in a leadership capacity, have to be fully and completely secure in who they are as women. You first have to ask yourself these questions:

- Do I fully grasp God's intention in creating me as a woman and not as a man?
- Am I completely Bible-centered in my theology when it comes to the specific roles within the church for women and men?

These questions are not easy ones, but they are of paramount importance when it comes to leadership of this kind, especially as it relates to the church.

There is no question that dignity and importance are attributed equally to both men and women in God's kingdom. In the very first chapter of God's Word, Genesis 1:27 lays to rest any notion of inequality; man is not better than woman, nor is woman better than man. From the very beginning, *"God created man in his image, in the image of God he created him, male and female he created them."* (Genesis 1:27) Men and women are equal in dignity and respect because God created them equally in His image.

Then we read on in verse 28, *"And God blessed **them**. And God said to **them**, 'Be fruitful and multiply and fill the earth and subdue it and have dominion over the fish of the sea and over the birds of the heavens and over every living thing that moves on the earth.'"* (Emphasis added) Men and women share in God's image; therefore, they share in the dignity and respect of that image. However, that does not negate roles within that image, and with those roles comes a certain order.

When Satan came to Eve in the Garden of Eden and seduced her into eating of the fruit of the Tree of Knowledge of Good and Evil, he deceived both man and woman into the greatest role reversal of all time. He knew that if he approached the woman, who incidentally only knew the rule concerning not eating of the fruit because it had been repeated to her by her husband, and made her the leader, then she would blame the serpent, the man would blame the woman, and they would be at odds for all time. And that's exactly what happened.

Notice that in Genesis 3:6, after the serpent had enticed Eve, Scripture records, *"So when the woman saw that the tree was good for food, and that it was a delight to the eyes, and that the tree was to be desired to make one wise, she took of the fruit and ate, and she also gave some to her husband **who was with her**, and he ate."* (Emphasis added) Further, Scripture records that even though Satan confused the order, God wasn't confused at all. He went straight to Adam to ask about the sin, not to Eve – even though she was the one who had been deceived into eating the fruit (Genesis 3:9). God intended His order for man's good, but Satan hates both God and man; therefore, he also hates God's order, so he went straight to the one tactic that would throw a monkey wrench into every single area of life. That unfortunately includes church leadership.

As I alluded to earlier in this chapter, many churches have abdicated even having a women's ministry leader because of the problems it has caused. Of course, the problems are due to sin, but the fact that sin is at the root of the problems doesn't mean we should eliminate this leadership position altogether. Instead, the sin itself should be eliminated by addressing it directly and effectively

It's my assertion that if women who feel a special call on their lives to lead the women in their church in a women's ministry would do so with a knowledge of roles and how they are ordered in God's kingdom, then we wouldn't have pastors who feel usurped and women who feel slighted. Instead, we would have unity and harmony within the church, where men assume the leadership role of the church, knowing that this leadership is healthy and unchallenged by women who simply want to support the leadership by ministering to the women in the special way that only women can.

Deborah knew this, and she exemplified it, even as a very prominent leader within God's community of believers. She absolutely did not usurp male leadership even as she led, and she beautifully demonstrates how this can be accomplished. We must have an attitude like Deborah's if we are going to step into a position like women's ministry leader. This attitude is to be one that understands God's order for gender roles yet does not discount equality in His kingdom.

2. She Recognizes God's Word as the Foundation

Women talk, and we talk a lot. Believe it or not, that is exactly the way God created us. We are relational and nurturing and care-giving, which are all also beautiful characteristics that embody our Creator. With the relational traits comes a communication trait, and that too is good. God designed it for good, and He intended it for good.

However, as I have acknowledged earlier, Satan hates God and he hates man. Consequently, he has made it his mission to use all that God intends for good to destroy us while we are here on earth. Our need to communicate our thoughts and opinions to others is one such area in which he tries to use our God-given design against us, especially with women in leadership.

It's a slippery slope when you have the ear of another. It's terribly tempting to convey your thoughts and ideas instead of God's. Granted, if we seek God first, our ideas will come from Him, but leaders must be very cautious here. After all, a women's ministry leader is leading women in God's kingdom and no other. Therefore it must be God's Word we speak and no other. Psalm 18:30 tells us, *"This God – his way is perfect; the word of the Lord proves true; he is a shield for all those who take refuge in him."*

Numerous competing ideas are out there, and many of them may sound good. They may even sound biblical. The only way we can be completely sure is to stay with God's Word. Deborah knew that, and she practiced that.

When deciding on Bible study material for your ladies, when deciding on retreat or conference topics or speakers, even when making decisions on events and more social functions, it is now your responsibility to be sure only God's Word is represented if you have taken up the mantle of leadership. This is a very big responsibility, to say the least, and certainly one that requires special attention.

Deception is subtle. It is subversive, and it comes out of areas where you will least expect it. Be wary. Be mindful. Be vigilant. But most of all, be sure that the only truths you speak, the only truths you allow, the only paths in which you lead your women are those reflected in the Bible. This is a characteristic of the women's ministry leader that cannot be compromised.

3. She Takes Courage as a Leader

It takes a special kind of person to lead women. We aren't easy to lead. If you don't see that, just ask any man! We are sensitive, caring, emotional creatures, but all of those positive qualities can lead to conflict and even contention. Sometimes conflict will arise between each other, and sometimes it may come from a disagreement with the men under whom we lead. Whenever conflict arises and from wherever conflict comes, a true leader is courageous under attack.

But where does this courage come from?

Courage must come from God, and it comes from Him when we know we are secure in Him. Deborah never flinched when the people came to her in fear over the impending attack by Jabin. The Bible simply says she immediately sent for Barak. She didn't hesitate, even though she must have surely known her life would be in peril – if not from the enemy, from those within her own country who opposed her efforts. She courageously acted, however, and hers was a courage born of identity. That's precisely why I began the enumeration of essential qualities for a women's ministry leader with being sure you know where your identity lies.

If your identity is first and foremost as a woman of God – a strong woman who leads – then in the face of certain adversity, you will find strength from the only Author and Giver of strength. If your courage is based on what you are without Him, then your courage will be fleeting, as will be your success. However, if your courage is rooted in Christ and Who He is and what He did for you, then dissent from anyone, including Satan, will not thwart you. This is the courage displayed by Deborah, and it is the courage necessary for a women's ministry leader. I believe she would sing with David as he sang in Psalm 18:39, *"For you equipped me with strength for the battle; you made those who rise against me sink under me."*

4. She Gives Glory to God

Once again, this is a battle against human pride, isn't it? Any time we are exalted to any sort of leadership position, our human tendency will move toward pride in our own accomplishments, as well as pride born from the praise of others. How do we combat this? We do just as Deborah did. We continually give all glory and honor to God – the Lord we serve and the Father we love.

It's indeed tempting to see the work we do, especially work in leadership, as a reflection of our accomplishments. It's tricky to stay safely on the right side of the line of recognizing our God-given talents without taking any credit for the work we may do because of those talents. As with every other area of our lives, once we submit to this role as leader, we also submit to the authority of God over our minds, and consequently, the mind is where we face this particular battle.

I believe Deborah understood this. She knew her own weaknesses. It's impossible to have hundreds, maybe even thousands of people come to you for counsel and wisdom and not recognize your human propensity toward pride. She had to have seen this, and in this knowledge, she demonstrated for us just how we do battle with pride: she made it a practice, in all things, to give God all the glory verbally.

Giving God the glory verbally is truly a matter of the mind's commanding the heart how to feel. If we fill our minds with God and His due glory, speaking it on every occasion and meditating on it as often as we can, then our hearts will eventually follow that knowledge and feel appropriately what the head already knows. Deborah spoke God's glory, and she did so at every opportunity afforded her. If you are feeling called to women's ministry leadership, then you are also feeling called to train your mind and your heart now to give God His due glory. Believe me, your flesh will want the glory for itself, and the only weapon you have to fight your flesh is the truth of God and His Word.

Think it. Say it. Meditate on it. Then feel it will all your heart. Your song will mirror Deborah's – in battle or in praise, and you too will hear the command, *"Awake, awake, Deborah! Awake, awake, break out in a song!"* (Judges 5:12)

5. She Embraces the Role of "Mother"

One of my favorite lines from Deborah's song in Judges 5 is in verse 7 when she sings, *"I, Deborah, arose as a mother in Israel."* I think those words are beautiful because she knew motherhood was beautiful. She didn't call herself "king" or "prophet" or "ruler" or even "leader," and a few of those would have been correct. No, Deborah sang that she arose as a "mother in Israel." She sang with thanksgiving and praise that she had been given the awesome privilege to nurture and care for God's people. Truly, this is the most important characteristic needed for any woman who is considering the job of women's ministry leader.

Leading a women's ministry cannot be about being in charge. I've seen far too many women long for this position simply because they loved giving out orders. I've also seen almost all of those ministries fail. It can't be about being a "leader," though leading is exactly what you will be doing. Once again, it's a matter of the heart. What does your heart want? What does it desire in taking this leadership position?

Sisters, if you are thinking about this position, your heart must be concerned for the nurturing of the women in your local church. Your heart must be about loving them, serving them, and in almost all cases, mothering them. A mother is knit to her children in ways that no other human being can comprehend, except for maybe other mothers. A mother wants only happiness for her children. She wants their safety and their well-being. She wants to protect them from all things that might endanger them. She will defend them with even her life, and she will be for them in everything they do. Deborah felt this way about the people for whom she ministered, and she sang about it in her praise for this privilege.

Before you move any further toward this very important job, please be sure that your heart for the women in your church is like the heart of a mother for her children. It cannot be about you or anything you might get out of it. It has to be motivated by a sincere desire to care for others, and that must include every aspect of that kind of motherly care. You must also understand that, just as a mother does for her children, you will be standing in the gap for them. You will get no accolades for this ministry. You must seek no accolades. Your reward must be only in seeing good come to those women, at whatever cost. Your care for them reveals your love.

Is God calling you to step into these sandals? Is He calling you to this new thing?

If I'm a Deborah, where Do I Start?

I hope that above all else I've conveyed in this chapter, I have communicated the seriousness with which you must approach this type of leadership. Women will look to you for guidance and for security, whether with meals and by hospitality or in Bible study and conferences. At the end of the day, the responsibility will rest with you. With that in mind, here are a few things you need to do if this is an area where you are feeling led:

• Pray. Pray. And then pray some more. Seek God out, asking him for wisdom and discernment as you move forward. He will guide you, both through prayer and through the reading of His Word. Seek Him first.

• Talk to the pastor or pastors in your church. If this is an area where God is truly leading you within the confines of your local church, your pastors will be in agreement with you. Be patient, however. It may not happen on your time schedule. Talk to them and seek their wisdom and guidance. God will not move in your heart without moving in theirs as well.

- If your pastors are in agreement, begin seeking out women with whom you can begin. You will need a team of peers to help you develop this kind of ministry. If one already exists in your church and you are simply stepping into a pre-existing role, seek out the women who are already involved. You will want them with you, giving feedback and helping you assess the needs of the women in your particular body of believers. Above everything else, remember that ministry is not a solo sport. If you are doing all the work, you are leading badly. On the flip side of that, if you are doing none of the work, you are also leading badly. Involve and train other women within the ministry.

- Once you have a team of women to help, begin to assess the particular needs of the women in your church. Look at the demographics. Are your women mostly older or younger, or is it a good mix? Are there existing meals ministries and hospital visitation ministries that may need improvement, or do you need to begin them? What kinds of Bible studies are already in place, or are there any? Each church is different, and each group of women will be different. Take the time necessary to see what your church needs. Above all, don't try to fit them into your mold. Remember: it's not about you. Assess what they need and then prayerfully figure out how best to serve them.

- After all is said and done, always refer to number four under the "Application" section: make all you do about God and His glory. If He is at your center, He will not let you fail.

God bless you as you prayerfully move toward serving the women in your church, in whatever way that may be.

Lydia

and the Small Group Leader

3

The story of Lydia is contained within two small verses of the Bible, Acts 16:14-15. Paul, Silas, and Timothy were traveling by the leading of the Holy Spirit, and according to His prompting, they went to the city of Philippi, a Roman colony and one of the leading cities of Macedonia. Once the men arrived in Philippi, they remained quiet, more than likely waiting for Saturday, the Sabbath. The first thing Paul always liked to do upon entering a new city on his missionary journeys was to go the synagogue.

However, Philippi had no synagogue, which reflected the lack of Jewish male leadership in this city. Jewish law required at least ten men to be present for the building of a synagogue, and since there was no synagogue, the logical conclusion is that there were very few Jewish men there. Paul and his companions did hear of a prayer gathering by the river, so they made their way there on the Sabbath. It was at this prayer meeting that they first met Lydia.

We can gather so much about this great woman leader, even in these two small verses, but also in a few other places where the Bible mentions her. What, however, can she teach us about this new thing? What can she show us about being a woman of God who is willing to step out and lead a small group of ladies in her home?

YESTERDAY'S FOOTSTEPS

LYDIA — the First Small Group Leader

1. Lydia — *an Industrious and Courageous Woman*

Lydia was a "seller of purple" from a place called Thyatira. The city of Thyatira was well-known for its purple dye, which had become very popular with the wealthy. This dye was extremely difficult to make because it was extracted drop by drop from a tiny shellfish known as a murex. Then merchants used this purple liquid to dye very expensive clothes for the wealthier members of society. Lydia probably learned this art in the land of her birth before later coming to Philippi, along with her entire household, to sell her wares.

The fact that Lydia was alone, unaccompanied by a man, suggests that she was a widow or had never been married. Either way, however, she was most likely wealthy. But understand that her wealth wouldn't have made it any easier on her within that society. Women were seen as second- and third-class citizens, no matter how much money they had. Most often, women were looked upon as slaves. For Lydia, along with her entire household, to venture out to another city would categorize her as a very industrious and courageous woman. No doubt the men in the city viewed her with disdain, and certainly any of the Jewish men did, though they seemed to have been in scarce supply anyway.

Her industry and courage, as they pertained to her lifestyle, were unquestionable, but they also were evident in terms of her gathering at the river to pray. At this time in history, women were not permitted to have their own beliefs. They were to believe as their husbands believed, and if not married, as their fathers did. That was one of the problems faced by Christianity for many in that society. Paul taught that in Jesus Christ there was no longer male and female, but all were one in Christ (Galatians 3:28). This teaching caused numerous problems because many women were converting to Christianity, and to the outside world, they were seen as unruly women – women who needed to be restrained or, in some cases, killed.

But here we have our Lydia, so courageous in her convictions that she led a group of women at the river to pray every Sabbath because there were no men to lead them. She obviously wasn't being secretive about it either since it seemed to be no problem for Paul and his friends to find her. Apparently, he simply had to ask where there might be those of the faith meeting, and they were pointed to Lydia's group by the river.

Lydia – both industrious and courageous – was just the sort of woman God might call to do a new thing.

2. Lydia ⁓ *a Woman with an Open Heart*

While still living in her hometown of Thyatira, Lydia had turned from her people's pagan beliefs and begun praying to God. What this tells us is that God had already moved in her. He had already plucked her out of that hell-bound race she was running with all her might and moved her toward Him. Her heart had been opened. When she moved to Philippi, she immediately sought those with like-minded devotion to God so that they could worship Him together.

None of those things happened because of human will. Lydia did not believe on the Lord and then eventually also on Jesus Christ because she was either weak- or strong-willed. All humanity is set against the truth of God. All humanity, at its core, is prideful and intentional in following after whatever makes the most of humanity. Moving after God, and especially God in Jesus Christ, makes the most of Him, not us. God had opened Lydia's heart, and she responded to His prompting.

How marvelous that God chooses ordinary people to do His work of advancing His kingdom! Lydia didn't know that the simple act of leading a group of women in prayer, even when societal norms would tell her that it was incorrect to do so in the absence of men, would lead to her conversion and the conversion of her entire household and that in her house the very first church in Europe would begin.

God uses simple people. He uses simple women by moving in a heart of humility and replacing that heart of stone with a heart of flesh. Then His great work is underway. Ruth didn't know that the diapers she changed for her baby boy, Obed, were the diapers of the boy whose lineage would bring the Christ. Adele Marion Fielde didn't know when she went with her new Baptist missionary husband to evangelize Thailand that he would die ten days later. She also didn't know that God had chosen her open and willing heart to continue anyway, eventually spreading the gospel all over China. Jackie Pullinger most likely never dreamed that God would use her to help, save, and restore hundreds of drug-addicted teens in Hong Kong, all in the name of Jesus. And Lydia, though probably a strong and bold woman, never dreamed that her open heart would be the genesis for a local church to be held in her home.

Further evidence that God had opened this wonderful woman's heart was her immediate response to Paul's teaching on Jesus. Her response to the truth was almost instantaneous. Luke simply records the following story in Acts 16:14-15: *One who heard us was a woman named Lydia, from the city of Thyatira, a seller of purple goods, who was a worshipper of God. The Lord opened her heart to pay attention to what was said by Paul. And after she was baptized, and her household as well, she urged us, saying, "If you have judged me to be faithful to the Lord, come to my house and stay." And she prevailed upon us.*

God used Lydia, just as he has used countless other men and women down through the ages, because their hearts were softened to hear His truth. He opens the heart, and once that miracle has been performed, obedient humility will be the starting point for great wonders on behalf of the kingdom of grace.

3. Lydia — *a Woman of Prayer*

Women can be such creatures of action. After all, God did create us to be the managers of the house, as Paul describes us in Titus 2, and any manager must be a doer. A manager has to be a person who can manage others, while making sure that every task is accomplished. Unfortunately, that can sometimes spill over into kingdom work. We see something that needs to be done, and we immediately get to the job of doing it. Lydia, on the other hand, demonstrates where a woman of action must lay her first priority – prayer.

One might suppose that it was a great disappointment for a woman such as Lydia to enter the city of Philippi, a great city of some importance, only to find that there weren't even enough Jewish men there to constitute a synagogue. Where would she pray? How was she going to fulfill the Law of Moses about keeping the Sabbath if there was no synagogue there for her to worship in? Prayer was obviously so important to Lydia that she was willing to step out in faith, even if it caused her trouble, so that she could pray on the Sabbath.

Most synagogues were built near water so that the ceremonial washing could take place. Lydia was intent on appropriate prayer as it had been taught her when she converted. She was so intent that she began a group not in her home, which might have been easier to keep quiet, but by the river so that the ceremonial washing could occur. Down by the river was a much more public place and sure to draw attention. Though Scripture doesn't mention any of these difficulties, it's not hard to imagine that she must have encountered some. After all, she was a woman leading women in prayer in public.

However, Lydia was a woman of prayer. She wanted communion with her Father above anything else, and she was willing to lead other women to following this same desire. Surely a woman like this is exactly the kind of woman God will call to do a new thing.

4. Lydia — a Woman of Bold Proclamation of Her Beliefs

Verses fourteen and fifteen of Acts 16 can tell us so many things about the character of this woman. We can easily surmise that she was bold in many areas. She moved her entire household to Philippi where she could do business more prosperously. The fact that she had a household to move says a lot, especially since no man is mentioned. She boldly professed her belief in God, so much so that she easily gathered a group of women who joined her every Sabbath day to pray by the river. It doesn't take a lot of effort to see that we are dealing with a woman of outstanding character. However, in her outstanding character, we also see a woman who wanted to tell others about the freedom she had experienced – first in God and then in God through Christ.

Lydia, with an open heart, listened to the words of Paul that Sabbath morning by the river, and she recognized that she needed this Jesus of whom He spoke. She wasted no time in accepting Jesus as her Savior and getting baptized on the spot as a proclamation of that new faith. Luke simply says in Acts 16:14-15, *"The Lord opened her heart to pay attention to what was said by Paul. And after she was baptized, and her household as well, she urged us...."*

This business woman, prayer leader, and bold proponent of her faith heard about and accepted Jesus, and her first instinct after being baptized was to tell her entire household about this new faith. Her reputation as a woman of integrity must have been tremendous since they were all baptized almost immediately. Most noteworthy was her immediate desire to tell those she loved about Jesus and to be sure that they, too, knew Him as their Savior.

But she didn't stop there. Right after that prayer meeting by the river, Paul and his compatriots found themselves in a Philippian prison after releasing a demon-possessed young slave girl from her bondage (Acts 16:16-34). Apparently, her owners had been making a lot of money off of her demonic ability to tell fortunes, so they had them arrested. Paul and Silas went to jail, where eventually, after an earthquake and an angel of the Lord freed Paul and Silas from their shackles, the Philippian jailor was also converted, along with his entire household. The magistrates eventually let Paul and his friends go because the city officials were embarrassed that they had unlawfully detained a Roman citizen. Look what Luke records in verse 40 of Acts 16 after Paul and Silas were released, *"So they went out of the prison and visited Lydia. And when they had seen the brothers,, they encouraged them and departed."*

What had Lydia been doing behind the scenes while Paul and his friends were in prison? She had been spreading the word about her conversion and about this new Christ of Whom she was learning. Thus, the first home church had begun. Lydia wasn't content to receive Christ and then sit on her laurels. No, she was so joyous at this new spiritual freedom that her instinct was to tell everyone she could find so that more and more people would come to know Him as their personal Lord and Savior. Only a few days after Paul and the others were carted off to jail, she saw them again, but this time when they came to her house, Paul was able to see all of the others who had come to salvation through her testimony.

Lydia was a woman who couldn't keep from telling others about the love of Christ that had permeated every single nuance of her existence.

5. Lydia — a Woman of Hospitality

The next thing Lydia did after being sure that everyone in her immediate vicinity knew about this Christ was to invite these men back to her home. At first glance, this may not seem like such a big deal. After all, it was definitely a custom of this time period to offer food and lodging to those visiting your area. However, many other factors were at play here, and Lydia's response with such a wonderfully kind deed and open hospitality are typical of the reaction that is necessary for the woman who is going to step out in faith and do this new thing.

Once again, we have to remember that Lydia was a woman on her own, something that was already looked upon by society as being under God's wrath. She would have known that. However, she never missed a beat when she invited Paul and his companions to come home and stay with her. Chances are really good that she wanted to hear more from Paul, to learn more about Jesus. But even beyond that, her open heart manifested itself further through her open home.

It's not easy to have guests. It couldn't have been easy to invite these strangers to come into her home without any preparation. It also couldn't have been easy to do so knowing the gossip that would surely ensue when she did. None of this mattered to our Lydia, though. As a matter of fact, the actual original language Luke used in this verse when recounting her invitation is important to note. She invited them, and then the last sentence of verse 15 reads, *"And she prevailed upon us."*

That word used here, "prevailed," has also been translated as "constrained." The meaning is a forceful one. Basically, Lydia wasn't taking no for an answer. They might have declined her offer out of consideration, but she would hear none of it. They were coming to her house, and she would be sure they were well taken care of. Once again, we see Lydia as a strong woman who was humbly allowing her strength of character to be used to the glory and advancement of God's Kingdom.

One of the necessary results of salvation is a changed heart, and it will be a changed heart toward good deeds. Good deeds don't save us, but once saved, we desire to obey our Father in the way of good deeds. Lydia opened her home, not only to Paul and the rest but also to many others so that the gospel could be shared. She shared her food and her life, not so that she could earn a reward, but because when the Holy Spirit enters a heart, He brings love, care, and compassion with Him. That's precisely why Jesus said in John 13:35, *"By this all people will know that you are my disciples, if you have love for one another."*

Lydia, a woman of means and character, was also a woman of hospitality and good deeds, and from her willingness to open her door to share with others, the first local church in Europe was born.

TODAY'S FOOTSTEPS

A Kind and Hospitable Small Group Leader

Opening your home to a group of women for fellowship and study of God's Word is no small undertaking. It requires a great amount of vulnerability and no small measure of trust that God won't leave you hanging. However, without small groups, churches often run the risk of having many members who just don't feel connected. Within the confines of the church service, there often isn't enough time to develop close, personal relationships that are necessary so that people feel safe to share the burdens of their hearts. Also, needs are left unmet, not because no one wants to help, but because no one knows to help. Having smaller groups meet outside of the regular church service provides much needed connections so that no one feels like just another number.

Additionally, although small groups with both men and women who share a commonality are very good, i.e. married couples, singles, parents, etc., there is a great need for groups of just men or just women. A certain level of fellowship and intimacy can only be met safely with people of the same sex, so these kinds of small groups are vital within any church.

However, who's going to lead them? Who's going to step out in faith and allow this group of people to meet regularly in her home? And even more than that, who's going to step into that kind of responsibility, ministering to a group in such a specific way?

Hopefully, when reading about Lydia, you have noticed some of the characteristics needed in a woman who wishes to lead a small group. Let's take a few minutes to take the traits outlined in Lydia's life to definitive and applicable measures, thereby enabling you further to decide whether or not this is the area of ministry to women that God is calling you to fill in your home church.

1. She is Courageous

We definitely have already seen this characteristic in our study of Deborah and the women's ministry leader, and we will no doubt see this attribute come up repeatedly. It takes definite courage to step out into any role of leadership, but we must be sure that the courage we seek is courage we receive from our Savior.

As with both Deborah and Lydia, their courage was somewhat borne of their obvious personalities. Both women were naturally bold. However, what set them apart as courageous women of God was their trust in God. Both women believed that whatever course of action their Lord required of them, He would stand in the gap for them, protecting them and the work they did on His behalf.

Bringing a group of women into your home and leading them in study and fellowship will require great courage. Even if they aren't necessarily meeting in your home, leading them is not going to be easy. It will require that you move under the anointing of the Holy Spirit and that you relinquish any sense of control you may think you have.

Courage for the believer isn't loud and boisterous. Courage for the believer is quiet and submissive. A woman who derives her courage from her Savior is a woman who doesn't need to be heard or to be right or to be the best. A woman whose courage originates in Jesus is a woman who might not know how things will turn out but who knows that in Christ, it will be good.

That's the courage we saw in Lydia, and that's the courage required for any woman to step out and lead women in a small group.

2. She has a Vulnerable, Open, and Loving Heart

Nothing is worse than walking into a group and immediately feeling as if you're not welcome. Unfortunately, that can be a prevalent issue among small groups, especially women's small groups. If the group has been together for a while or if most of the people in the group know each other really well outside of the small group setting, a newcomer can feel like an outsider pretty quickly.

Now this may seem harsh, but this is fully the responsibility of the small group leader. A group will follow the lead of its leader. If the leader is kind and open to everyone, the group will follow suit. However, if the leader appears closed off and emotionally unavailable, the members will appear the same way.

In the same vein, if the leader of a small group isn't vulnerable with her own heart and her own struggles, then she certainly won't be able to expect those ladies in her group to be, and when they do want to share, it may seem like an unsafe environment.

Lydia's heart was open to the Holy Spirit's prompting. She was obviously so well out of her own way that when the Spirit spoke, she not only listened, but sprung immediately into action. Hers was most likely an easy home to be in, an easy environment in which to feel welcome, unjudged, and loved. These characteristics are of paramount importance to leading any small group, but because women tend to be so much more emotional than men, it is particularly important when leading a small group for women.

3. She Knows the Importance of Prayer

Small groups can go haywire pretty quickly. The intentions can sometimes start out really well, but a few misplaced words, too much "chat" time, not enough Bible, and before you know it, your group is more of a social gathering that a small group Bible study.

There is only one foolproof way to keep that from happening, and Lydia knew this from the onset: everything must center on prayer. A woman who feels led to begin a small group study in her home must be a woman whose prayer life is sound and continual. This woman knows her Father's voice, and she communes with him on a daily basis. Then when it comes time to have the group meet, she doesn't even have to plan for prayer. It's such a natural part of who she is that the group will also become a group of prayer.

Another, more urgent reason for being a woman of prayer exists when you step out into leadership in this way. The devil won't like it. He doesn't want you to be an agent of deeper fellowship with our Savior. He hates the idea of your love and compassion and hospitality furthering the kingdom of God. Consequently, every step you make in this realm requires inordinate prayer coverage. Beseech your friends and family to pray on your behalf. Be sure that the members of your group recognize going in that you are a woman who not only values prayer but who lives prayer. This is your line of defense against a formidable, though ultimately vanquished enemy. Lydia knew this, and she exemplifies this for small group leaders everywhere.

4. She has a Heart to Speak the Truth

One of the things I love most about Lydia is her immediate response to salvation: she told her household, and they followed her example. Then she told the entire town, and a church was born in her home. She was so overwhelmed by what had been done for her on the cross of Calvary by her Savior that she couldn't keep quiet about it. She wanted others to know, so she told them.

So many Christians have deluded themselves into saying things like, "I just don't have the gift of evangelism." To that I would ask, "Were you given the gift of salvation? If so, how can you keep that in?" No one is advocating that every believer has to be on a street corner with a sign that says "Jesus Saves," but I am acknowledging that a person who has truly received the gift of salvation and understands what she has received will not be able to keep that a secret.

Taking that a step further, I want to refer to what I wrote a few paragraphs up about being vulnerable. A woman who feels led to lead a women's small group should also be a woman who feels secure about sharing the gift that her Savior has freely given to her, and I mean all aspects of that gift. A leader is the most effective when she is transparent. A leader is the most compassionate if she is vulnerable and willing to share her own failures and shortcomings, not to draw attention to those but to shine a beacon on the grace and mercy of Jesus!

There is no place for pride in true Christian leadership. It's prideful to think hiding your failures makes you more appealing as a leader. Sisters, if you want to take on the awesome responsibility of leading a small group of women, do so in humility and vulnerability. You will pave the way for so much healing, and consequently, the attention will be rightfully off of you and onto the great Lord and Savior we should exalt in the first place.

5. She Displays the Great Gift of Hospitality

What a misunderstood gift this one has grown to be! I remember being in a small group one time when one of the ladies very sweetly told me that the one thing she appreciated about me was my gift of hospitality. I asked her what she meant by that since I knew I struggled in this particular area. You see, I'm from the South, and inasmuch as that is true, I've been trained from a very young age that the way we appear is sacred. Hair, make-up, clothes, house, children, husband – all of it must appear together and perfect. Consequently, I'd grown to abhor having people over to my house for fear that it wasn't perfect enough. I knew this was wrong, so I was struggling, and I was interested in what she meant.

She said exactly what I thought she would say. She said she loved coming over to my house for functions because everything always looked so wonderful. She enjoyed the food, and she said that my house always seemed so inviting. I appreciated hearing that, but in my heart, I knew that was not the gift of hospitality. The gift of hospitality is wanting to open your home, not dreading it and working so that all of the appearances are perfect.

It was some weeks later when I was able to come back to that group and share what I had been struggling with. I confessed my shortcomings in the area of hospitality and asked my fellow small group members to help hold me accountable to truly being hospitable, not just appearing so.

Lydia was hospitable because inviting Paul and his friends over wasn't about showing off her home. She obviously wasn't stressing about everything being perfect before they came since she hadn't even had time to go home and check. She simply had a home and was happy to share it with others, especially as it advanced the kingdom of God.

I remember thinking that evening after the young lady told me she thought I had the gift of hospitality that there were other women whom I knew that really had it. "You can use my home any time you need to for youth meetings," one lady said. "I may not be there, and it may not be clean, but I'll show you where I keep the extra key." Now that's the gift of hospitality!

If you are feeling led to begin a small group, check your heart. How do you feel about letting people in, and I'm not necessarily referring just to your house right now. This is an aspect, once again, of humility. Not about you. Always about God.

If I'm a Lydia, where Do I Start?

Although still a daunting task, leading a small group can be an easy and very enjoyable experience. It's extraordinarily important that you first ascertain if you do indeed have the right mindset before leading one, but if you have prayerfully considered everything entailed with this undertaking and still feel this is where God would use you to minister to women in your local church, here are a few suggestions as you move forward:

- Pray. Once again, this one will be first on each starting list. We simply must begin any movement toward leadership by seeking out our Father and His will for us first. Pray about what kind of group God wants you to lead. Pray about how He wants you to go about it. Pray about the subject matter. Pray for the members, even before you know who they are. Pray, pray, pray.

- Talk to your pastor or pastor(s). This one, too, will be one you will see each time. I cannot stress enough that to go against God's appointed leadership within your church is to go against God Himself. He has set a hierarchy of authority, not to constrain us but to liberate us from our own fallen tendencies toward sin. Trust your pastors and consult with them. If your church doesn't have an organized small group ministry, then you will need permission to begin something like this. If God is moving in your heart, he will be moving in theirs, too. If your church already has a small group ministry, your first step may be to contact the person in charge of that ministry. You do not want to begin something for God's kingdom in such a way that might offend others within God's kingdom. Follow proper chains of authority and speak to whomever you must before starting anything.

- Once you have the go ahead to lead a group of women, begin looking for study material. Again, if your church already has an existing small group ministry, you may be led to a set of materials that is pre-approved. If not, prayerfully consider your choices. Try to find something that will meet the needs of the demographics of your group. If at all possible, look for things that are written with women in mind, but don't be limited by that. Above all, check everything first before ordering multiple copies. Make sure that the content is scriptural and in line with your church's teaching. If your pastor or ministry leader is willing, have him or her look through anything before you order copies for everyone else.

- Set a time and place and invite some women!! A good small-group size should rarely exceed twelve people, but you should try to begin with five or more. If not, where two or more are gathered...! Begin and end with prayer, move into study time, then fellowship and snacks (if you desire). If you aren't going to rotate meeting places, snacks are a good way to get everyone involved. Have a sign-up sheet at the meeting so that people can take turns bringing goodies.

- End with prayer and request-sharing time. Please be sure to build this into the schedule of your small group time. Depending on the size of your group, it might be advantageous to also pass around a "Prayer Request" sheet and begin a prayer chain. Whatever your process, allow your members time to both be prayed for and to pray for others. Prayer is a necessary parenthesis to any small group meeting, so beginning with it and ending with it is very important.

Now just relax! Everything won't be perfect. Sometimes your meeting may go too long or too short, or sometimes you may feel like you just didn't handle certain things well. That's okay. No one expects you to be their all-knowing president or especially their come-to-the-rescue savior. You are a humble servant seeking to minister to and serve the women in your church in the best way you can. God will honor that, and the ladies will be blessed by it.

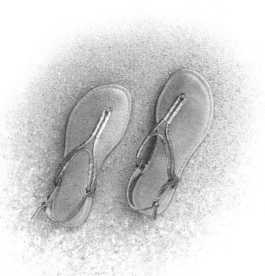

Elizabeth

and the Mentor

One of the most beloved stories in the Bible is found in the second chapter of Luke, for this chapter tells of the birth of our Savior. No child has been through even a few sessions of Sunday school without having heard the stories surrounding the virgin birth of Jesus: Mary's visit from Gabriel telling her what was going to happen and Joseph's visit from the angel telling him how he was to respond.

However, if we back up just one chapter, we read another wonderful story – one that precedes the birth of Christ, that actually foretells His glorious birth, and that sets a precedent for one of the most beautiful woman-to-woman relationships ever recorded. The relationship between Mary, the mother of Jesus, and her cousin Elizabeth, the mother of John the Baptist, is where I wish to take us as we explore the ministry of mentoring, especially as it relates to women mentoring women. Paul calls it "training" in Titus 2, but in the family of Christ, mentoring is a vitally important, yet often overlooked ministry within the church.

Often as I travel around the world teaching women's conferences, ministering to women, and sharing the truths necessary so that women are not isolated or alone in Christ, I hear women ask for someone to mentor them. I often receive calls from younger women who ask me to recommend someone to mentor them, even though they may not use that particular word.

The funny thing is that I also hear from older women who complain about younger women. "They won't listen," they say, or "They think they know too much," or "They have no respect for their elders." Among that group of detractors, not one time have I had one of these older women come to me and ask to mentor someone else. As well as hearing the complaints, I have heard women say that they don't feel equipped to mentor or guide another woman, but no one is asking if they **can** mentor.

It's not hard to see this issue, is it? With the occasional exception, younger women are wanting mentors, but older women don't want to or don't think they can mentor them. Consequently, these younger ladies who are looking for guidance and wisdom are sent to counselors or psychologists or small groups or pastors.

Turning away a young woman looking for help would have been a completely foreign concept in Elizabeth's day. On the other side of the issue, it would have been unusual for Mary not to have sought an older woman for counsel. No one in either of those situations would have considered seeking a third party to intervene. Mary knew to go to her older, wiser cousin, and Elizabeth knew to listen and guide her younger charge. Period.

The truth is that there is a very strong biblical premise for mentorship – both being one and seeking one – and this is a vast area of need in our local churches today. What drove Elizabeth and Mary to come together at perhaps the greatest moment in the history of mankind? Why was the way they went about seeking each other both God-honoring and God-glorifying?

Their relationship reveals a perfect example of another opportunity for women today to step out and do a new thing.

YESTERDAY'S FOOTSTEPS

ELIZABETH — a God-Honoring Mentor

Luke began his narrative on the birth of Jesus with two miraculous conceptions: Mary, a virgin in her early teens, and Elizabeth, an old married woman most likely in her 70's or 80's. Both of these miracles were preceded by a visit from Gabriel, and both conceptions were indeed miraculous. And understand, miracles didn't happen anymore in that day and age. There hadn't been a single miracle for over 400 years. There hadn't been a series of miracles for over 500 years. No one had heard from an angel or from God in well over 400 years. When Mary was visited by Gabriel, she needed to tell someone. She had heard that her cousin Elizabeth had miraculously become pregnant in her old age, so Mary knew that Elizabeth was the one she needed to seek out. Consequently, Mary left immediately. Mary needed to speak to someone she trusted, who would both listen to her and guide her in the way of the Lord. How very wise it was for this young girl in a precarious situation to seek an older woman.

And Elizabeth wasn't just any older woman. Not only was she Mary's cousin, but she had also been born into a family with a long lineage of priests. Her husband, Zechariah, was a priest, and Elizabeth knew the Lord. Luke says of her and her husband in Luke 1:6, *"And they were both righteous before God, walking blamelessly in all the commandments and statutes of the Lord."*

No doubt Mary and Elizabeth had a close relationship prior to the events listed in Luke Chapter One, so Mary knew immediately that she should seek out this older, righteous woman of God. Mary decided to make the 75-mile journey from Galilee to Judah so that she could seek the wise counsel of her godly cousin, Elizabeth.

1. Elizabeth — *a Woman Filled with the Holy Spirit*

According to Scripture, Elizabeth was barren when the angel Gabriel visited her husband as he took his turn serving as the priest before God in the temple. Gabriel promised Zechariah that Elizabeth would conceive in her old age and give birth to a great prophet. And indeed, it was so. Zechariah returned home, and Elizabeth conceived, though she kept the pregnancy a secret for the first six months.

After that first six months, Gabriel then visited Mary and announced to her that she, too, would conceive miraculously. Since Mary already knew about her cousin's pregnancy, we can gather from Scripture that very little time had passed between when Mary found about Elizabeth's pregnancy and when she, herself, became pregnant. The Bible tells us that Mary immediately went to Elizabeth.

Once Mary got to the village in Judah where her cousin lived, they greeted one another, which would have meant that they sat down and exchanged conversation about health, family, etc. It was during this conversation that we read in Luke 1:41, *"When Elizabeth heard the greeting of Mary, the baby leaped in her womb. And Elizabeth was filled with the Holy Spirit."*

Please understand that this was no small statement. Basically, Mary was recounting to Elizabeth all that had happened to her, and this righteous woman recognized the magnificence of what she was hearing. Don't let the integrity of her character slip by unnoticed in this small sentence. Of course, the Holy Spirit can and does speak to us when He desires to do so, but Elizabeth was so in tune with her Father and His Word that when she heard these words and felt her baby move, she knew immediately that it wasn't just the normal kicking of her growing baby inside her. She knew at precisely that moment that her baby's movement was due to the joy brought about through the Holy Spirit at what was transpiring before her eyes.

The truth is that anyone can pretend to be righteous and worthy of the role of mentor. But only a woman filled with God, a woman whose life has been consistently in honor of Him and His Word, will recognize the importance of such an occasion without prompting. Elizabeth was truly a woman worthy of guiding her young cousin in this momentous occasion.

2. Elizabeth — *a Woman Who Confirms God's Word*

At this point in the narrative, one might stop to ask why. Why did Mary go to Elizabeth? Why was this visit one of such immediacy? What was Mary hoping to find out by visiting her cousin? And why Elizabeth?

Well, if we back up to when Gabriel came to Mary, we'll see that what he tells her in this vision is simply mindboggling. She was a child, barely in her teens. She had known no man, though she was betrothed to Joseph. And yet this heavenly being was telling her that she would conceive and bear a son, but not just any son – the Son, the Messiah – and all of this would take place without human intervention. What was she supposed to do with this information?

God never leaves us hanging, does He? I love the fact that even though we might mistakenly think that He has, He never does. Notice what

67

Gabriel adds in Luke 1:36-37 before he leaves Mary, *"And behold, your relative Elizabeth in her old age has also conceived a son, and this is the sixth month with her who was called barren. For nothing will be impossible with God."*

If ever there was a character trait necessary for a woman to effectively minister to another woman in such an intimate way as mentorship, that trait must be that she is a living confirmation of the Word of God. And that's exactly what Elizabeth was. She was the living embodiment that God was still in the business of doing miracles, His having done so already in her own life. How gracious of our Father to tell young Mary of Elizabeth's miracle pregnancy as Mary undoubtedly wondered what she was supposed to do with the information she had been given.

God intended for Mary to go to Elizabeth, a godly, older woman who would not only counsel and guide her in the words of their Father, but also confirm God's very Words in the life that grew within her.

3. Elizabeth ⁓ *a Giver of Blessing*

When Elizabeth exclaimed that the baby in her womb had leapt for joy at the words of Mary, she was overwhelmed with gratitude and beautiful humility. She could have doubted Mary. She could have remained aloof, taking on the air of authority as one fifty or sixty years Mary's senior. She could have kept her emotions in check for the sake of station and propriety. But Elizabeth didn't do any of that. Instead, she was so far removed from any human concerns that she was overcome with the joy that can only come from humble service to God.

Luke records her saying in 1:42-45, *"Blessed are you among women, and blessed is the fruit of your womb! And why is this granted to me that the mother of my Lord should come to me? For behold, when the sound of your greeting came to my ears, the baby in my womb leaped for joy. And blessed is she who believed that there would be a fulfillment of what was spoken to her from the Lord."*

Elizabeth is a wonderful example of a woman so God-centered and God-focused that she responded, even in the moment, with only Him at her center. She didn't think of herself, other than to be overwhelmed that she was even included in this occasion, and she only thought of uplifting the young girl in front of her. She confirmed the words of Gabriel, and then she went on to confirm in Mary all that the Lord had revealed to her. Remember that Elizabeth was from a rather respected family and was of considerable means within her community. Yet in the midst of this situation, Elizabeth thought only of praise and blessing, concerning both the situation and her young cousin. Surely this kind of humility and God-centeredness made Elizabeth the perfect example for women who are called to mentor other women.

4. Elizabeth — *the Woman Who Cares*

The next point about Elizabeth's character as it relates to her qualifications as a mentor might slip by unnoticed if we aren't careful. After Mary sings her famous praise of God's faithfulness, Luke 1:56 simply records, *"And Mary remained with her about three months and returned to her home."*

Mary remained with Elizabeth for three more months, which, coincidentally, were the final three months of Elizabeth's pregnancy. Given her advanced age, that last trimester could not have been easy. It would have been very understandable for Elizabeth to send Mary home rather quickly after she had blessed her and encouraged her. After all, caring for herself would have been a full-time job, without adding a young teenage girl who was pregnant and not married into that mix.

Apparently, Mary didn't stay to help with the delivery either, so that can't be why she remained for those three months. She left, and then Luke records the birth. No, I believe Elizabeth most likely encouraged Mary to stay so that the older, wiser cousin could continue to uplift and encourage Mary for as long as she could. It wouldn't have been easy. More than likely, Elizabeth felt pretty horrible toward the end, and I'm also sure that Mary was a help to Elizabeth. But how many women would have been that dedicated to seeing Mary's guidance through under such circumstances?

It's quite obvious that Elizabeth wasn't a flash-in-the-pan kind of mentor. She was in it for the long haul, and she would encourage and guide Mary for as long as she possibly could. Once again, the character trait that stands out is humility, along with being other-centered as opposed to self-centered.

5. Elizabeth — *the Loyal Wife*

Finally, when this pregnancy came to an end, another very important quality becomes evident in this great woman of God. She stood by her husband even when it might have been easier to give in to the pressure from others.

Zechariah had lost his ability to speak after his encounter with Gabriel in the temple. Since Zechariah had questioned how this miraculous conception could take place given the advanced age of both Zechariah and his wife, Gabriel told him he wouldn't be able to speak until the baby was born. However, before leaving, Gabriel did tell Zechariah that he was to name the baby John. Of course, Zechariah would have relayed this information to Elizabeth when he went home, but he wouldn't have told anyone else. She didn't even reveal that she was pregnant until six months later.

However, on the day of the child's birth, Elizabeth did have a son, though Zechariah still had not regained his voice. It wasn't until the eighth day after the baby's birth, when he was to be circumcised, that the time came for Zechariah to regain his voice. Relatives and neighbors had come to celebrate this glorious day. They were happy with Zechariah and Elizabeth that God had granted them a child in their old age.

But just as Zechariah had surely told Elizabeth the reason he had lost his voice, he must have also told her that he would regain his speech once the child was born. Yet he remained silent. Wouldn't it have been easy for Elizabeth to also doubt that John should be the boy's name? The people present at the celebration were pressuring her to name the child after his father or, at the very least, after someone in her family. They pressed and pressed, and I can only imagine that most other women might have begun to doubt. Her husband's voice hadn't returned, so maybe he had heard the name wrong, too. But not Elizabeth.

No, our character-driven mentor would not be moved. Instead, Luke records her firmly answering their forceful requests in 1:60, *"No; he shall be called John."* Her friends and relatives started questioning her too, and then they went directly to Zechariah. He asked for something to write on and confirmed that the boy's name was indeed to be John. At that very moment, his voice returned.

Truly there are many lessons we can take away from these few verses, but one attribute that screams out is Elizabeth's loyalty to her husband, even when many others would have faltered. Her loyalty to Mary, to Zechariah, and ultimately to God is an example of the traits that make her the perfect example for any woman who feels the call to take up the mantle of mentoring within her local church.

TODAY'S FOOTSTEPS

A Spirit-Filled Mentor

A deep, vacant hole exists in most churches when it comes to older women mentoring, guiding, and ministering to younger women. And please understand here, I am not necessarily referring to age, though years do bring experience. What I am speaking of is the need for women who are still moving through life's struggles and trials to have more mature, seasoned Christian women come alongside of them. I've had young women come to me in tears over the lack of seasoned women in their church who were willing to counsel them. Ladies, this should not be the case for a myriad of reasons, not the least of which is that it isn't biblical for older women to neglect the mentoring of those who are newer in the faith. However, this deficit of mentors certainly should not occur since we have a plethora of women in the Bible who serve as wonderful examples on how to be such a woman.

With that in mind, let's take few minutes to explore Elizabeth's characteristics and make some practical applications for seasoned Christian women to use in pursuing this much needed area of ministry in the local church.

1. She is a Spirit-Filled Woman

At the risk of misleading anyone reading this book, I am not referring to being "filled with the Holy Spirit" in the sense of that which occurs at salvation. Nor am I referring to the continual filling we all experience every day as we battle with our sin natures. When D.L. Moody was asked why he needed to be continually filled with the Holy Spirit, he replied simply, "Because I leak!" We do leak, so we should always seek our Father and His Word throughout every day, thereby being continually filled with the Holy Spirit.

However, that's not what I'm talking about. I'm talking about being a woman who is so filled with the Holy Spirit – a woman who is continually re-filling her tank that leaks – that when she is approached for wisdom in any situation, it's the Holy Spirit's wisdom that comes out, not her own.

This woman knows the value of spending daily time with her Father in prayer, study, and meditation. This woman has experienced the beauty of knowing that by doing so she is training her mind to respond in the Spirit and not in the flesh.

Stepping into the role of mentorship is not a light step. It is very, very heavy. When any person comes to you for spiritual counsel, you are representing God to them. You are helping them see life's situation through a "God lens," if you will, through the lens of God's Word. You are helping them practically apply holy principles to their lives. And God will hold you accountable for that. Not a light step. Very, very heavy.

Elizabeth was a woman who knew the Lord, but even more than that, she was a woman who lived out what the Lord spoke. This is the first and foremost qualification for a woman entering this kind of ministry in her local church.

2. She Speaks Words that are Confirmed by God's Word

A woman who is mentoring other women cannot place too much emphasis on this trait. We see this characteristic played out very practically in the life of Elizabeth. Elizabeth's first words to Mary were a confirmation of what the angel Gabriel had said to her that night. Her words confirmed what God had already said.

Giving advice can be a very slippery slope. Not inserting yourself into the mix can be really difficult sometimes, and not inserting what the world says is even more difficult. Every word uttered in the mentor relationship must be perfectly aligned with God's Word. Every piece of advice you give, every word of praise or comfort or consideration that comes out of your mouth must be expressed exactly as God has said it in his Word. The only way a mentor can be certain that she is doing that is to know what God's Word says, which is why we started with number one – being filled with the Holy Spirit.

There are no shortcuts here. If you are feeling led to move in this area of ministry, you absolutely must be a woman of the Word. You must be filled with God's Word so that every word you speak is a confirmation of what God has said.

3. She Speaks Words of Encouragement

We are by nature a self-centered people. Granted, some people are more selfish than others, but selfishness is a part of who we are at our cores. Self-centeredness and pride were at the root of the very first sin in the Garden of Eden, and they remain mankind's greatest obstacles. This self-nature will also be your biggest obstacle in serving in this particular ministry unless you are careful.

It's a heady thing to have someone look up to you the way a young woman will when you are her source of wisdom and advice. When your words are the ones she clings to and follows, you will find it relatively easy to get lost in your words. Elizabeth never once said a word that lifted herself above that of her young charge. On the contrary, she blessed Mary, speaking words of encouragement to her, even as she surely spoke words of instruction and sometimes even rebuke.

Once again, the issue here is being fully God-centered and Holy Spirit-filled in every aspect of your life. Only then will you be qualified to minister to another in this way. Everything is about your Father, and therefore, everything is about how you glorify Him in your words and in your counsel. Being Spirit-filled is not a personality trait; it is a discipline. It requires discipline, and it requires a continual refilling of your leaky spiritual tank.

4. She's In It for the Long Haul

People go to other people for advice all of the time. They do it at the water cooler at work, in the line at the grocery store, or on the kids' soccer field. Women ask their friends, their neighbors, even their ministers for advice, and that is often a good thing. However, there is a definite difference between seeking advice from the occasional person and seeking someone to mentor or guide you as we are speaking of this type of ministry. And there are loads of differences between handing out the occasional piece of advice and committing to a young woman in this manner. It is just that – a commitment.

Notice that Elizabeth, though probably in her 70's or 80's and six months pregnant, did not send young Mary away. She let Mary stay with her for three months, right up until the time came for Elizabeth to give birth.

I'm convinced it wasn't to utilize the young Mary to help around the house, though I'm sure that did occur. I'm convinced that Elizabeth was invested in her young cousin. She loved her, but even more than that, she recognized the deep responsibility given her to guide and counsel and support Mary. She was committed.

Agreeing to mentor and guide a young Christian woman is no easy task, and it will take your time – a lot of it! The decision to accept such a challenge should be weighed and measured because it takes not only tremendous responsibility, but also tremendous commitment. However, if this is truly an area where God is calling you to serve the women in your local church, then meeting with them and talking to them will be a delight, not a burden. It will lift your heart, not weigh it down. What a joy to invest in the kingdom of God by investing in the next generation!

5. Her Priorities are in Order

I end here because I want to stress this one so much. No one can offer to help put another's house in order if her own house is in disarray. That's just a fact. That's not to say that everything in the mentor's life is perfect; that's simply impossible. However, it is necessary that she is doing all that she can to serve her own household well. I believe Elizabeth's example is a tremendous one because of the way she stood by her husband's decision to name their baby John, even though he couldn't speak to explain why and even though the relatives were pressuring her to do what was actually more acceptable according to custom. Elizabeth stood firmly by her husband, which absolutely qualified her to counsel young Mary in the ways of womanhood.

I realize that this is not a popular concept in mainstream society. The common thinking is live and let live. What's right for you is what's right for you. Why, America was founded on slogans like "Don't Tread on Me!" We are a people who prize their individuality and independence, which consequently makes us a people who do not like to be told what to do. And we don't like to be told that there are standards which must be met before we can do something. Unfortunately, however, this is exactly the case with ministering to women on a long term basis.

How can I counsel a woman on marriage if mine is not a priority in my life? How can I give any guidance on raising children if I haven't invested in my own? How can I minister to a woman concerning godly living when I don't practice the same principles? Again, it doesn't mean every aspect of our lives has to be perfect in order to mentor. As a matter of fact, failures in these areas often make us more viable in terms of advice. But what is necessary is that we are on the other side of those failures, humbly willing to share what we have learned in the process. That's what makes this ministry helpful: experienced women sharing with younger, less experienced ones.

Simply put, clean your own house before offering to pick up someone else's mess.

If I'm an Elizabeth, where Do I Start?

John Piper wrote an excellent book called *When I Don't Desire God: How to Fight for Joy.* In it he wrote the following: "One of the challenges I repeatedly hold out to the people of our church – especially the women – is that they make it one of their aims to age into a sage. I love the vision of older women full of seasoned spiritual fruit that comes only with long life and much affliction and deep meditation on the Word of God. So many younger women yearn for older women, who are deeply wise, to share the wisdom God has taught them over the years."[2]

Mr. Piper's words describe exactly what a mentor is, but notice that becoming a mentor begins with a desire to move in this way, using all that God has taught you in your life to help another. And then it takes commitment; it takes discipline. If this is an area of ministry in your local church where God is leading you to step out, here are a few suggestions on where to begin:

- Pray. See, I told you. This one will be first every time. Seek the Lord diligently as you take steps toward this ministry. Once again, the enemy won't like it. As a matter of fact, he will hate everything about your decision. Be prepared for that and pray continually before you make another move. Then just wait. God is getting ready to pave the way!!

- Build relationships with younger women. The younger ladies in your church need to get to know you first. They will not approach you to speak with them unless they first see that you are approachable. Join a small group where there are younger women in attendance. Volunteer in the nursery or the preschool department at church. Let them see you, know you, and talk with you. If God is truly calling you to this very important ministry, the door will open for it to begin.

- Take a leap of faith and ask a younger woman to coffee. Better yet, take her coffee while she is at home, most likely taking care of a house full of children. Listen to her; befriend her. The relationship may or may

[2] Piper, John, When I Don't Desire God: How to Fight for Joy, Wheaton, IL, Crossway, 2004. Print

not lead to mentoring, but it might. At the very least, you will have a new friend.

• Never stop studying God's Word. Never stop meditating on it. The Bible is your schoolroom. It is your training ground. Making the Bible a part of everything you do is of paramount importance while you prepare for this kind of ministry.

Mentoring young women is a beautiful, often less-sought-out ministry. It will receive no commendations, no accolades, and very few acknowledgments. But that's just here on earth. It is, however, extraordinary in the eyes of our Father. He is honored in it, and He will bless you through it. May the Lord keep you and grow you as you move in His will for your life, seeking to step in the sandals that will bring Him glory.

Dorcas

and the Servant Disciple

A very popular Christian comedian does a bit about the different jobs available in the church. He makes tongue-in-cheek reference to those who can't do anything else as having a "servant's heart." He says that if all else fails, they can always stack chairs. Even though he is actually poking fun at the prideful heart that equates servanthood with a lack of intelligence, the hidden meaning is often lost on the church community. Stacking chairs, making meals, and distributing clothes have become the tasks for menial Christianity, often overlooked for more sought-after areas of ministry, like teacher or leader or singer, making the definition of the most meaningful Christian service as the service most seen, the service most visible in the public eye.

God couldn't disagree more, and the Bible couldn't take a more opposite view of meaningful Christian service. As a matter of fact, Jesus was quite explicit when He addressed His own disciples in this area, *And they came to Capernaum. And when he was in the house he asked them,*

"What were you discussing on the way?" But they kept silent, for on the way they had argued with one another about who was the greatest. And he sat down and called the twelve. And he said to them, "If anyone would be first, he must be last of all and servant of all." (Mark 9:33-35)

This is precisely why the woman called to the ministry of service within her local church, especially service to the women in need there, will be counted among the first in the kingdom of God. It is entirely unfortunate that a call to this type of service would need to be listed among the new things to which God is calling us, but society has made it so. And there is probably no better example in the Bible of a woman fulfilling such a ministry in her local church than Dorcas from Acts 9.

YESTERDAY'S FOOTSTEPS

DORCAS ⁓ a Giving and Kind Servant Disciple

The story of Dorcas, or Tabitha as she was called in the Hebrew language, is found in Acts 9:36-43. Within this very short passage that documents Peter's missionary journeys after the Day of Pentecost, we find the most explicit and beautiful illustration of a life lived fully the way Jesus described to his disciples in Mark 9. For any who are feeling led to minister to women within their local church in this manner, I say God bless you. God bless your humility, your industry, and your fortitude.

There are great rewards for those who answer this call, but as with the other calls to ministry, certain qualities are necessary for the one venturing into this particular area. After all, we are human, and our humanity necessitates the propensity for sin, even sin in service. Therefore, let's take the time to recount the ways in which Dorcas exemplified a woman called to minister to other women in her church through service.

1. Dorcas ⟶ *the Disciple*

Acts 9:36 introduces this woman of God in this manner: *"Now there was in Joppa a disciple named Tabitha, which, translated, means Dorcas."* (Emphasis added)

This is the first and only feminine use of the word "disciple" in the entire New Testament. It is wonderful that Dorcas receives that honor. To be a disciple of Christ, one must follow His teachings, His ministry, and His ways.

Dorcas' conversion was further evidence that the gospel had spread after the Day of Pentecost. She lived in Joppa, a seaport town on the cost of the Mediterranean Sea. Many of the thousands who were saved at Pentecost were Grecian, and it would have been these believers who spread the word about Christ up and down the coastal towns. Dorcas most likely heard about Jesus there in Joppa from one of the converts from Pentecost, and thereafter, her life became solely committed to His mission.

That's a disciple.

The opportunity to be a disciple of Christ is not limited by gender, gift, nationality, or race. A disciple of Christ is one whose life is fully dedicated to all that Christ is, all that He stands for, and all that He teaches. The fact that Luke describes Dorcas as a disciple should set to rest any misconceptions that public ministry is more viable in the eyes of God than servant ministry. One might argue that the opposite is true, and Dorcas was living proof of this fact.

2. Dorcas ⁓ *a Woman Full of Good Works and Charity*

Dorcas was indeed a wonderful, wonderful woman. She was, in effect, the actual embodiment of all that a Christian should be. Acts 9:36b states, *"She was full of good works and acts of charity."*

She was full of good works and acts of charity. The actual Greek rendering of that word translated as "full" is worth mentioning. Ephesians 3:19 uses that word when Paul wrote that we should *"...know the love of Christ that surpasses knowledge, that you may be filled with all the fullness of God."* The concept Luke is conveying concerning Dorcas is the same idea that Paul was expressing in Ephesians – to be completely dedicated to something or totally controlled by something. Dorcas was literally controlled by her life of doing good for others, namely in making clothes for them.

The word used in Greek for what Dorcas was doing was *eliamosunai*, from which we get our word for "nonprofit organization." Dorcas ran one of the first nonprofit organizations, which means she didn't make money from her wares. She gave them away. She lived to serve and provide for others. This desire quite literally controlled her. In short, the life of Dorcas was the absolute definition of what Christianity is to be.

3. Dorcas ⁓ *a Woman of Action*

Most translations of Acts 9:36 add the words "which she did" after saying that she was a woman full of good works and acts of charity. "Which she did." How often is that left out of the equation! Sometimes I wish I had a dime for every instance when a woman came to me with some idea or another about service, especially this type of service, yet that idea never came to fruition. These women were full of "good ideas," not necessarily "good works," and that's not because they are awful women. They just lacked the fortitude necessary to turn these good ideas into good works "which they do."

The truth is, that in order to be a disciple of good works like Dorcas, we have to be willing to put our own needs and wants on hold. Life becomes about the service, not the convenience of the service. You can be sure that Dorcas had to put herself on the back burner many, many times as she served. Her name means "gazelle" or "graceful," which has led many commentators to assume that she was beautiful and lovely, yet it seems that she devoted her life to the service of others instead of to herself. Whether she was a widow or had never been married isn't really the issue. What is the issue is her diligence to be a doer of the word, not just a hearer (James 1:22).

4. Dorcas — *a Woman Dearly Loved*

Luke records that Dorcas became ill and died. Traditionally in that society, death and the process of preparing the dead was an immediate act. The ceremonial washing and preparations required tampering with things seen as unclean, so they generally went about this process speedily. However, Acts 9:37 says, *"In those days she became ill and died, and when they had washed her, they laid her in an upper room."*

Why wouldn't they finish the process? Why would they complete the ceremonial washing and then put her in a room? The answer is quite simply because they knew Peter was in town. They loved this woman so much that to part with her was unthinkable, so they did the unthinkable and didn't bury her. This is a testimony both to their extraordinary faith in God and His ability to raise the dead to life and to the tremendous love these women had for their dear Dorcas.

When Peter arrived in the upper room, he was met by many women weeping over their friend's death. They showed Peter all of the beautiful clothes Dorcas had made for them. They were devastated that she had been taken from them.

Their statements tell us so much more about Dorcas than the fact that she was skilled in sewing and had the fortitude to use her skill to do something about the clothing needs of others. She was also obviously a remarkably loving woman. To inspire this kind of grief and this type of response clearly indicates that she was a woman not only of service, but also of endearing love.

Paul reminds us in 1 Corinthians 13:3 and 13, *"If I give away all I have, and if I deliver my body to be burned, but have not love, I gain nothing. So now faith, hope, and love abide, these three; but the greatest of these is love."*

5. Dorcas ⁓ *a Life of Revival*

Luke records one of the most spectacular miracles ever performed after the Day of Pentecost. After sending the mourning women out of the room, Peter simply said, "Tabitha, arise," and the beautiful disciple of God arose. The days of decay and deterioration that undoubtedly had taken place in her mortal body moved backwards, like the hands of a clock, and cells were rejuvenated, atoms reborn. What a miracle!! Peter immediately presented her to her friends, and oh, how joyful they must have been! Luke simply records in verse 42, *"And it became known throughout all Joppa, and many believed in the Lord."*

Those women to whom Dorcas had ministered her entire life must have left that place singing and praising the Lord. An amazing revival took place in that city, and as Luke wrote, *"Many believed in the Lord."* In other words, many would live forever. Many had their sins instantaneously washed away by the blood of the Lamb. Many would see their Savior in paradise and live for eternity as His bride. Many were saved, and they were saved because one woman lived a life devoted to loving service in such a way so that when she died, the people whom she served simply didn't want to live without her. They wanted her back, and so they called for Peter to pray for her resurrection.

And many believed.

Dorcas could not have known during her very simple life in this simple seaport town that her acts of charity and kindness would result in the wonderful revival that occurred in Joppa that day. She couldn't have known that every time she put needle to cloth, every time she accepted no payment but delivered her beautiful robes free of charge, each made with the loving hands of a disciple of Christ, that each of those seemingly miniscule moments would lead to a day when many would believe. Truly, her life was the perfect example for a woman who feels called to be a servant disciple, especially as it pertains to the women with whom she worships in her local church.

TODAY'S FOOTSTEPS

A Giving and Kind Servant Disciple

It's understandable that for some, a woman like Dorcas is intimidating. Some of us have a hard time making our beds in the morning, much less making clothes for someone else or even making a meal that is even remotely edible. That's why God is a wonderful and multi-faceted God. He doesn't hand out just one gift, and if you don't have that one gift, you're out of luck. Isn't He wonderful? No, God hands out many different kinds of gifts, and most people have more than one. The gift of being a servant disciple is just one of many gifts.

However, I stand by my premise that it is perhaps one of the most important gifts, in that when it is shared, the one sharing it is emulating true Christianity. Consequently, if you have a special talent of helps – if you are an excellent cook or chef or seamstress or quilter or good at cleaning and homemaking – then perhaps God is calling you to this very special and much needed ministry from women to women in your church.

Once again, let's break down these qualities of ministry that we see in Dorcas into applicable attributes so that you will have a knowledgeable basis upon which to make a decision. However, and this is important, every single one of us should hear and answer the call to serving one another in this very practical way. If meals are needed, you should sign up to help, even if it just means you are calling the pizza delivery guy to take them dinner.

Serving one another isn't optional. We are all called to that. That said, it's still a viable question to ask if you are called to this specific ministry as the focus of your place in ministering to women in your local church.

1. She Lives as a Disciple

Although being a disciple is something to which every Christian is called, it must be a priority when a Christian desires to move in some type of formal ministry. Good works are only good as they are unto the Lord and to His glory. Being a disciple before we launch into this kind of service is exceedingly important in order to keep those priorities straight.

For example, there is no shortage of existing philanthropic organizations that do a myriad of good deeds in the world today. Food, medicine, water, shelters – all of these and more are represented all over the world in the name of humanitarian effort, and many of them help. However, a Christian is called to a much higher task before giving even a piece of bread to a starving individual. If those works are accomplished outside of Christ, then they may seem good in the short term, but what is being done about a person's eternity? As Isaiah reminded us in Isaiah 64:6, *"We have all become like one who is unclean, and all our righteous deeds are like a polluted garment."* In other words, without Christ, we're operating only in the temporal instead of the eternal, and the eternal must be the priority when we are serving others in any way.

Like Dorcas, moving toward a service ministry in your local church requires that you live fully centered on Christ in every aspect of your life. Dorcas was described as being "full" of good works, and the only way a person can be utterly controlled by the desire to serve is if she is first filled with Christ.

2. She is "Full" of Good Works

All of these points naturally bring us to the next practical application, and that is our motivation. Why do you want to serve? This may seem like a silly question, but the answer will determine whether one is dedicated to service or to being recognized for service. The first is a motivation born out of discipleship, and the second is a motivation born out of a need for affirmation.

In order to ascertain your motivations and have the ability to interpret why you want to move into this kind of service ministry, quite a lot of honest introspection is required. What drives you? When you do something for someone else, are you hurt or angry if you are not recognized for that service? Can you honestly say that doing for others brings you joy, or is your joy a derivative of their response to your service? These are truly difficult questions, and no one is expecting you to share your answers. However, you know what the answers are, and more importantly, so does God.

Dorcas was a woman fully motivated by a desire to serve as unto her Lord, Jesus Christ. The words that Luke uses to describe her, as well as the reaction of the women when she died, give testimony to that fact. This woman was motivated by a sincere desire to serve, and that is really the only kind of person who should presume to make this type of ministry her own.

3. She has a Heart and Life Ready to Act

Like Dorcas, a person moving into the ministry of servant disciple must be in a season of her life where that is a logical possibility. It may be that you want to serve in this capacity, but you are in the middle of a family crisis, you have several young children still at home, or maybe you are dealing with a serious illness that might preclude your action. In other words, be practical with what you can do at this point in your life as opposed to what you might like to do.

Obviously, Dorcas was in a position in her life where she was able to dedicate her time in service to others. No husband or children were mentioned in the passage, though that certainly doesn't mean there weren't any. However, she was wise enough to know her own limitations, not promising to do things she either wasn't prepared to do or wasn't in a position to do.

Be realistic, but be humble in your realism. God can and will do all that is necessary to give you the time and energy to do any ministry to which He calls you. Although we can't allow our situations and circumstances to limit God, we also must be wise concerning the circumstances in which God has sovereignly placed us at any given time in our lives.

4. She is Kind and Loving

Have you ever had someone do something for you that should have made you feel loved, but the person doing it was so unlovable that you simply couldn't receive the act properly? It's very difficult to accept an act as a genuine response to love when love doesn't seem to be the motivating factor in the person's act of giving.

Dorcas was a woman dearly loved, and the love was not simply a result of her good works. The good works were a result of her truly loving spirit, and loving her in return was a natural response. The point is this: unless you develop a heart that truly cares for the women to whom you wish to minister, then those acts of service will never point to Christ. He is a Savior driven in his actions by his extraordinary love for us. What we do for others, therefore, must be driven by our love for them, and that has to be apparent.

Love must be the determining factor and motivation behind all that we do. You may know how to bake a mean batch of cupcakes, but your cupcakes are only going to offer empty calories if the only thing people see is the "mean." Before you venture into a servant disciple ministry, be sure you have the heart of a servant disciple. Otherwise, as Paul put it, your acts will be no more meaningful than a clanging cymbal. (1 Corinthians 13:1)

5. She Leaves Behind a Legacy

The word "legacy" has been so misused in today's society that even using it in the context of a Christian's service to Christ is a sensitive thing. A "legacy" by definition is what you leave behind when you are no longer in the picture. Dorcas quite literally left behind a legacy of salvation. Her life brought many to know the Lord, and then her death and resurrection did so even more!

What are you going to leave behind when you have gone home to heaven? How are people going to remember you? Once again, these seem like simple questions, but they really aren't.

For example, if you were to take on a ministry such as the one Dorcas had, would you be remembered for the amazing desserts you made, or would you be remembered for the way Christ shined through you each and every time you made them? Would you be remembered for making the most beautiful quilts on earth, or would you be remembered for having a spirit that brought Christ-like warmth with every quilt you delivered? How will people remember you? What will be your legacy?

These are questions to ask yourself now, before you begin such a ministry, for in the answers you will see what motivates your desire to serve in this capacity. Pray that the Lord reveals to you whether yours is a heart like that of Dorcas, a heart that serves so that others see Christ, not the gift or the giver.

If I'm a Dorcas, where Do I Start?

On the surface, stepping into these particular sandals may seem like an easy thing, but nothing could be further from the truth. This servant disciple ministry brings with it great responsibility, but if done correctly, it also brings with it so very many blessings. If God has gifted you with a certain skill or craft and you sense His urging to make this your ministry to the women in your church, here are a few suggestions to begin:

- Yep, you guessed it – pray! Seek your Father for the wisdom and discernment necessary to serve women this way. You will be put in situation upon situation where you will be the only Jesus some people may see that day. Generally, meals, clothes, blankets, and house cleaning are things women need when some tragedy has befallen them or life has thrown them a few too many curve balls. While yours will be a service that will bless them in the physical sense, the opportunities you will have to be a blessing to them in the spiritual sense must not be overlooked. Time conversing with your Father will ready you for each and every occasion.

- Study and meditate daily on God's Word. No ministry can move forward without these two practices. After all, you will be serving others in the name of Jesus. You must know this great Savior Whom you represent. You will need Him as much as those you serve will need Him, so do not neglect to spend time in His Word as you prepare.

- Build relationships with the women in your church. If there is an existing women's Bible study or small group, be sure to get involved. Volunteer to greet or to work in the nursery or the children's ministry. Anywhere that women gather, make it your mission to be there. By getting to know them and, more importantly, by letting them get to know you, a bridge of trust will be forged. When they are in need, they will think of you and call upon you for help. However, if they don't know you, they also won't know to call you. Get out there and be known!

- If there is a prayer ministry in your church, be in it. When things happen to the women in your church where they would need a servant disciple, generally they will seek prayer. If you establish yourself rightfully as a woman of prayer, you will be trusted as a woman of service as well.

- If your church is big enough, recruit others to help you. Your goal shouldn't be to carry the weight of the servant disciple ministries on your own, but to allow others with the same gifts to help too. Often what's missing in churches is an organized ministry of helps. If one exists, join it. If one doesn't, pray about starting one (after consulting your pastors first). Remember that Christianity means family, not lone rangers, but a family working together to serve one another.

May the Lord bless you and keep you as you pray about this very important and necessary ministry in God's family.

Hannah

and the Prayer Warrior

Robert Murray M'Cheyne, a great preacher who lived in the late nineteenth century, once said, "What a man is alone on his knees before God, that he is and no more."[3] How very true. Prayer should be like air for the believer, yet it is often seen as more of a last resort than the very sustenance we need to survive. Prayer is the very way we converse with our Father. It is the way in which power is generated in the heavenly realm, and it is one of the manners by which God has ordained His will to be done. Consequently, once we take on the ministry of praying not only on our behalf but also on behalf of others, we have moved in a power best understood in its fullest. After all, Jesus said with the right amount of faith, we can move mountains (Matthew 17:20).

Are you ready to move into the most powerful of the "new things" to which God is calling His women today? Are you ready to become a woman so entrenched in the power and majesty of conversation with our God that

---

[3]Cited by: Matthew, P.G. "The Effectual Prayer," http://www.gracevalley.org/sermon_,trans/2001/Effecutal_Prayer.html

your ministry, most especially to the women in your local church, surrounds them with the beautiful love of God?

If indeed you are considering these sandals as those you wish to wear in your ministry to women in your church, then it is truly worth your time to consider Hannah from 1 Samuel 1-2. Often she is studied in terms of the prayer she prayed in 1 Samuel 2 in thanksgiving to God for giving her Samuel even though she was barren. But what can we learn of her character that might aid us in determining our own qualifications for ministry in this area? Truly, we can learn much from both her attitude of prayer as well as her attitude as she approaches her prayer.

YESTERDAY'S FOOTSTEPS

HANNAH ⁓ An Obedient and True Prayer Warrior

Hannah was the wife of Elkanah, a Jewish man from the hill country of Ephraim. We can read about Hannah in the first two chapters of the first book of Samuel. It is worth taking special note of this woman because of the place God has given her within His Word. Not only are her life and struggles given quite a bit of air time, but God included her prayer – word for word – in the pages of the Bible. If we were to study this woman for no other reasons, these two would be enough. However, so much about her character and the way she responded to adversity and disappointment points indiscriminately to a solid and wonderful example for any woman wishing to make prayer for her sisters her special ministry within the church.

1. Hannah ⁓ *Obedient to the End*

Hannah was the wife of Elkanah, but Elkanah took a second wife. Unfortunately, Hannah was barren, and though Elkanah loved her dearly, he seemed to lack spiritual insight into this problem. Instead of seeking God for a miracle, as Rebekah and Sarah had experienced in Jewish history, he sought a human solution to the problem and took another wife. Just as with any time we try to find solutions to our problems by human means, Elkanah ended up with very human consequences to his decision. There was no peace in his home.

Elkanah's other wife, Peninnah, did bear him children, but Peninnah wasn't content simply to have heirs for her husband. Apparently, she also found cruel pleasure in tormenting poor Hannah over her inability to conceive. All of them would have been familiar with passages like the one in Deuteronomy 7:13a, which read, *"He will love you, bless you, and multiply you."* Peninnah would have tormented Hannah on the basis of her barrenness, claiming that she was cursed and not blessed.

Additionally, Elkanah didn't understand Hannah's pain and sorrow, seeking to quench it with gifts. Hannah wouldn't be comforted by her husband's ill-suited attempts. She was sickened at heart and in utter despair.

I cannot imagine that their yearly trip to Shiloh was on her top ten list of things to do in her despair. The trip was a long one, and it must have afforded her rival, Peninnah, countless opportunities to torment her along the way. Hannah had faced years of disappointment in her barrenness, but still she traveled, year after year, to worship the God Who remained silent against her pain. Her obedience to God and to His covenant was not influenced by her circumstances.

Truly, it wouldn't have been surprising for us to read at this point in the story of dear Hannah of her asking to be excused from this annual trip, but we do not. As a matter of fact, the story does not skip a beat between explaining her sorrow and making the pilgrimage to Shiloh. At the very onset, Hannah is an example to all of us of a woman dedicated to worshipping her Father, even when she doesn't understand His ways.

2. Hannah ⌐ *Boldly Seeking God*

Once they arrived at the festival, it seems as if not much time passed before Hannah went into the tabernacle to pray. Please understand that no one else was in the tabernacle, except for Eli, the priest, because they were all out at the festival, eating and drinking. Scripture tells us that Hannah got up from the festivities and went into the tabernacle to pray.

Here is a woman whose life was in despair. She was at a festival in honor of the God Who had not answered her prayers, and what was her response? She went to Him in prayer. Hannah decided to step out from the outer court of festivities and into the inner court of petition. Hannah, right in the middle of her pain and torment, took her relationship of faith with her Lord from situational to personal, from weeping to petition, from victim to victorious. What a testimony of a faithful woman whose character was shaped by faith and not by circumstances.

That certainly didn't mean she wasn't sad. She absolutely was. 1 Samuel 1:10 says, *"She was deeply distressed and prayed to the LORD and wept bitterly."* Boldness before the throne of grace doesn't mean hypocrisy. Boldness, as displayed beautifully by Hannah, simply means petitioning in humble purity of heart. Her faith, though shaken, was not defeated. She continued beseeching the Lord in her distress, even leaving the celebration of every other person in Shiloh to come before her Father.

Hannah's relationship with God was one exemplified by openness. It was personal. It was real. And it was bold.

3. Hannah — *Trusting in God*

One of my favorite verses, as it applies to Hannah, is in 1 Samuel 1:18. Hannah had been praying so fervently to God, doing so in the recesses of her heart so as not to make a show, that the priest, Eli, thought she was drunk. He told her to go away and to, in essence, sober up. She quickly told him that she had not been drinking but that she was simply praying with all her heart, in "great anxiety and vexation." Eli recanted his impulsive and incorrect assessment, blessing her and asking God for her prayers to be answered. Verse 18 simply says, *"Then the woman went her way and ate, and her face was no longer sad."*

Wow! We don't know how many years had passed during which Hannah had been unable to conceive. We only know that it was long enough for Peninnah to have given birth a few times, so it had to have been at least several years. Nothing anyone could do would comfort her, including the obvious favored attention from her husband. However, once she came to the Lord in ardent prayer, pouring her heart out to Him, she was uplifted. She quite literally was no longer sad. How could that be?

My sisters, this is the faithful response of a woman who believes in the power of prayer. She didn't go before God hoping He would answer her. She didn't fall on her face before the throne of grace just in case He might be listening. No, Hannah went into that tabernacle, laid her requests before God, and then left with the weight of those burdens no longer on her shoulders. She left her cares on the altar. Hannah lived out what the Apostle Peter taught in 1 Peter 5:7, *"Cast all your cares on him, because he cares for you."* She also lived out what the psalmist wrote in Psalm 42:5, *"Why are you downcast, O my soul, and why are you in turmoil? Hope in God; for I shall again praise him, my salvation and my God."*

Hannah prayed in trust, not that her prayers might be answered. She prayed in trust that her prayers would be answered, so she was therefore able to rise from her knees and go away burden-free.

4. Hannah ⁓ *Keeping Her Promise*

Hannah's prayer to God was a specific one. She not only asked that He grant her a son, but she also vowed that upon His answering of this prayer, she would give her son to God's service as soon as he was old enough.

Scripture records that Hannah, Elkanah, and the rest of that family finished their worship time in Shiloh and then returned to Ramah, where "in due time" Hannah did conceive and bear a son to Elkanah. We do not know how much time is "due time," but the intimation is that it wasn't necessarily immediate. Some time passed, but God was faithful to His promise and answered Hannah's prayer for a son.

Understand that Hannah had no other children. Can you imagine how much this little boy must have meant to her? He was the actual embodiment of answered prayer, yet she knew that she must keep her promise to God and give the boy to Him in service.

An amazing testimony to Hanna's character is the fact that she didn't try to get out of her promise. Scripture doesn't record Hannah's going back to God to try to bargain her way out of this situation, though we must assume that her return trip to Shiloh was probably one of the most difficult trips she had ever made. This time she had to leave her precious son with Eli, a priest of questionable character, along with his two despicable sons. But Hannah never faltered. She never wavered. She was a woman of her word, a woman of kept promises, and she was sure to give to God what she had promised to give.

Once again, this is another point at which we can see the phenomenal character of Hannah. Her trust in God was so complete that even though she was going to be leaving her son in somewhat questionable hands, she never questioned God. She never doubted Him. Her faith is certainly something that can be upheld as an example for women of prayer everywhere.

5. Hannah ⁓ *Praising Her God*

However, even beyond her obvious faith in God that allowed her to leave Samuel in the care of Eli, what she did next is simply astounding when we really look at the situation. She sang a song of praise to God that is so prolific that it has become a model for prayer for God's people ever since. Hannah brought her only son, along with new clothes she had made for him in which to serve in the temple and everything she would need to offer appropriate sacrifices, and instead of going away wailing, as I know I would have done, her very next words were, "My heart exults in the Lord!"

She goes on for ten more verses, singing God's praises, extoling Him in His majesty, His sovereignty, His omnipotence, and His love. Here she is, leaving what is likely the most important thing in her entire life, knowing that she will only see him once a year for the rest of his life because of her promise to God, and instead of bemoaning her situation, Hannah once again shows us what a real woman of faithful prayer looks like.

A woman like this is a woman who praises God and trusts Him no matter the circumstances, because she knows that God has proven Himself faithful over and over again. She knows He will not falter now, and her response is simply to praise Him.

Her song proclaims that God is her salvation, *"My mouth derides my enemies, because I rejoice in your salvation."* (1 Samuel 2:1b) Then she declares her God's holiness and His omniscience, *"There is none holy like the LORD; for there is none besides you...for the LORD is a God of knowledge, and by him actions are weighed."* (I Samuel 2:2, 3b) And she sings of His perfect care and His sovereignty, *"There is no rock like our God...He will guard the feet of his faithful ones. . .The Lord will judge the ends of the earth; he will give strength to his king and exalt the power of his anointed."* (I Samuel 2:2b, 9, 10b)

Hannah responded to every circumstance in her life with prayer, with both praise and petition, and neither circumstances nor people were a hindrance to her diligence. Her prayerful responses are truly an example of the character needed to be a serving woman of prayer.

TODAY'S FOOTSTEPS

An Obedient and True Prayer Warrior

Prayer is a personal expression of our relationship with our Father and with our Savior, Jesus Christ. However, there are times when the power of prayer is needed in exponential terms, when the situation is so dire or the problems so immense that we either don't have the words to pray or we don't even know where to start in our prayers. What happens in your church when a woman is so overwhelmed by life that she simply needs someone to lift her up in prayer? Do you feel a burden to make this your particular ministry? Is your heart quickened at the idea that you might be the one who stands in the gap for these women whose hearts are shattered over their present circumstances?

Truthfully, all Christians are called to be a people of prayer. Prayer is power, and it is communion with the Father. However, the command to all Christians to pray doesn't negate the unique calling of some in the church to intercede on behalf of the saints. That woman who has the ministry of being an intercessor for the women with whom she worships in her local church has a special ministry indeed.

Hannah certainly emulates the character of such a woman, and it behooves each of us to learn exactly what kind of woman should enter into such an important and holy ministry as being a prayer warrior for the women in her church.

1. She Possesses a Language of Obedience

Any woman wishing to enter a ministry on behalf of the women in her church has a definite responsibility as it pertains to her own life. Is her life characterized by obedience, or is it characterized by rebellion? A woman wishing to lead in any way must have a life that is unquestionably reflective of a heart of obedience.

Now certainly that doesn't mean that her life is perfect. If that were the prerequisite, then ministry would be a vacant place. What it does mean, however, is that her life is characterized by obedience. That is, she seeks to do her Father's will, putting its priority above all else in her life.

Possessing the discipline of obedience is particularly true of the woman whose call is in intercessory prayer. A woman who stands in the gap on behalf of anyone, in this case the women in her local church, must be a woman whose mind is disciplined and whose heart is trained to respond to God. A woman feeling called to this vital ministry must be absolutely in tune to what God expects and what He desires from his children.

Her prayers will be driven by her heart first, so her heart must be driven by God's law. His commands were not given to constrain or contain us, but to give us freedom to live as a people unencumbered by the cares of this world. When in prayer, the woman who is interceding will best be led by a heart that is first led by obedience to God. Hannah exemplified a woman with an obedient heart, and this is an uncompromising requisite for this prayer ministry.

2. She Comes Boldly Before the Throne of Grace

How do you view prayer? Is it a drudgery? Is it something that is to be done in the morning when you put in your required quiet time? Or do you see it as a beautiful communication between you and your Lord? Hannah very obviously saw it as a time of interaction with God, a time when she could pour her heart out to Him without fear of reproach, where she could faithfully and trustingly expect Him to hear and to answer. This is the necessary attitude for the woman who desires to do this not only for herself, but also for others in formal ministry.

You see, it's all about perspective. When you pray, God is listening. He's never further away than your first glance upward. He never changes. He is constant. What may possibly change is your perspective on the reality of what occurs when we pray. Angels sing and the heavens rejoice when a saint beseeches her Father. If she doesn't rest in these prayers, reality doesn't shift. She simply operates outside of what is.

Realizing the paramount importance of prayer, the prayer warrior views reality as it is and is not influenced by the limitations of the human psyche. Prayer is heavenly communication, and the warrior who understands the brilliance and majesty of this communication is the warrior who approaches the throne of grace boldly and without compunction.

How do you view prayer? The way you answer this question might very well be the one answer that should determine whether this is, in fact, the ministry you should seek in your church.

3. She Moves in Holy Trust

Just like with number two, your answer to the question posed there will apply here: how do you view prayer? Hannah never wavered in her belief that God was listening and that He would answer her. Your view of God will often determine what you think about His answers.

The prayer warrior must emulate David. David prayed with boldness, and Hannah sought God out like this man after God's heart. *"I love you, O LORD, my strength. The Lord is my rock and my fortress and my deliverer, my God, my rock, in whom I take refuge, my shield, and the horn of my salvation, my stronghold."* (Psalm 18:1-2) The prayer warrior doesn't question whether or not God has time for her or if He will pay any attention to her. The prayer warrior knows that her Father wants to hear from her, that He delights in her petitions and requests. Like David, can you pray with this kind of confidence?

If you cannot trust that God is listening and will answer your prayers, how will you be an effective advocate on behalf of others? This is a question that bears answering for any who wish to enter into this most holy of ministries: do you trust God to answer you when you call?

4. She Keeps Her Promises

James wrote in James 5:12, *"But above all, my brothers, do not swear, either by heaven or by earth or by any other oath, but let your 'yes' be yes and your 'no' be no, so that you may not fall under condemnation."* One of the most prevalent issues in today's society is the lack of truth telling.

Unfortunately, many of us have decided that a lack of following through with something we said we would do is not lying. James would disagree with that. As a matter of fact, he even went so far as to say that we should remain true to what we say we will or will not do to avoid "condemnation."

That's serious language.

Hannah exemplified honesty in the extreme, in that she kept her word to God, even at great personal pain. Today many women have a hard time keeping their word to each other. Although this is a character trait that all of us should strive for, it is one that should most especially be sought after by the one who is praying, i.e., speaking to God on behalf of another.

Sharing prayer requests is a vulnerable thing. When you are moving in ministry in this particular fashion, you are asking that women trust you with their innermost struggles. If you have not proven yourself trustworthy in something so menial as keeping your word, how might you expect someone to trust you with their communications before God?

May we all make our "yes" be yes and our "no" be no, but for the one wishing to wage war in the spiritual realm on behalf of her fellow sisters in Christ, let this be a trait she strives for even more.

5. She is a Woman of Praise

I've heard it said that attitude is everything. Well, it isn't everything, but it certainly is something. Hannah showed us what it looks like to be a woman who sees God's majesty, His sovereignty, and His glory in every situation, and she definitely exemplifies what this character trait must be for the prayer warriors in our churches. After all, if you don't proclaim how amazing this God you are petitioning is, how much faith do you really have?

A woman moving in this type of ministry must have as her mantra passages like Romans 8:28, *"And we know that for those who love God* all things work together for good, for those who are called according to his purpose." Or Jeremiah 29:11, "For I know the plans I have for you, declares the LORD, plans for welfare and not for evil, to give you a future and a hope."

This woman of prayer knows He is a faithful God and that He will never leave nor forsake His children. Therefore, the woman called to this ministry will praise Him in all circumstances, knowing that His love and sovereign care supersede the very fabric of all we see. He is fully in control, and in recognizing this control, the woman moving as a prayer warrior on behalf of her sisters in Christ displays this speech of praise above all else. This woman will sing with Hannah, "My heart exults in the Lord; my strength is exalted in the Lord."

If I'm a Hannah, where Do I Start?

Certainly prayer is to be an essential part of every Christian's life. However, the office of prayer warrior, sometimes referred to as intercessory prayer, is a blessed and wonderful addition to ministry in the local church. All of us are called to pray, but some are called in a unique way to pray on behalf of others.

Women ministering to women in the local church is a beautiful thing, and this office of prayer ministry is such a necessary one. Are you feeling led to make these the sandals you fill? Is this the new thing God has for you in service for the women in your church? If so, here are a few suggestions to get started:

- Of course, prayer is first on the list, and I know you will be engaged in that, but pray intentionally that God would open your heart as each prayer need becomes known. Pray that He would develop in you a sensitive spirit to the needs of others, even when they can't put words to those needs.

- Build relationships with the women in your church. In order to know how to pray for them, you must know them. Many mistakenly think that this particular ministry means you can be a loner. Some will even point at the less social women in their church and assume this ministry would be a good fit for them. Nothing could be further from the truth! A prayer warrior must have a relationship with the people for whom they are planning to pray. Even more than that, women have to know you in order to trust you with their prayer requests. You can build these relationships by volunteering in different places, i.e. nursery, children's ministry, youth ministry, as well as joining any ladies' small groups or Bible studies already in place.

- If a prayer ministry exists in your church, join it. If one does not, pray about starting one (after speaking with your pastors, of course). It will be so reassuring to the women of your church to know there is an organized group of women ready, willing, and able to pray for their needs.

- Find some good resources on prayer and read them. Timothy Keller has written an excellent book on prayer simply called *Prayer.* I highly recommend it. Whatever your choices, read up, but it would be a good idea to approach one of your pastors to recommend a book to you. That way you are sure to read something in line with your church's doctrine and beliefs.

• Start making a daily or weekly prayer list. Become organized in your own prayer life so that once it expands to include others, you already have a system in place. Again, there are many resources out there to help you with this. *Before Amen* by Max Lucado is one excellent resource, but again, ask one of your pastors and follow his recommendations first. For the more techy women, there are also many apps available now to help you get organized. Explore your options, but above all, have a plan. God will move you and your circumstances so that you will be ready as your ministry grows.

Hannah knew what it meant to have a character suited to being a prayer warrior. Know God, talk to Him, trust Him, and be obedient to Him. If these are areas where you are strong, and prayer is already a regular part of your relationship with God, then a prayer ministry for the women in your local church might be exactly the area to which God is calling you to look to Him. He will do a new thing, and it might just be through you!

Priscilla

and the Teacher

I have purposely left for last the role of teacher in the ministry of women to women for a number of reasons. One significant reason is the seriousness of such a call on any life, especially as it relates to women, since there is so much controversy within Christian circles on whether or not women should teach.

James wrote, *"Not many of you should become teachers, my brothers, for you know that we who teach will be judged with greater strictness."* (James 3:1) When a person teaches the Word of God, that person is quite literally representing God's words and how they should be both interpreted and applied. This is a weighty responsibility and one that must not be taken lightly. As a matter of fact, James clearly states that those who presume to teach will be judged more strictly. That is, they will be held to a higher accountability because their words will influence others about God's Word. A teacher has a listening audience, and that audience will naturally be influenced by what the teacher says. If a teacher represents

God incorrectly, so as to lead someone astray, the teacher is the one who will be held responsible for that before God.

When speaking of the children standing in front of him, Jesus said in Matthew 18:6, *"Whoever causes one of these little ones who believe in me to sin, it would be better for him to have a great millstone fastened around his neck and to be drowned in the depth of the sea."* Since Jesus had said just one sentence earlier that we are all to be like children in our faith, it must be assumed that what He says about teaching things that lead children astray must also be applied to teaching any believer.

Teaching is serious business. I have run into many women who think they feel the call to teach, but in reality, they feel the call to have a microphone in their hands. They will be held accountable at the same level as those whose call is sincere. Teaching is an area where women truly can and should minister to other women within their local church, but it is also a pathway where few should tread.

It's serious.

If I am coming across very heavy here, please know that my words are intentional. I feel the weight of this responsibility each and every time I step behind a podium. Tens, hundreds, sometimes thousands of attentive ears are listening to the way I present God's Holy Word, and I appropriately feel the weight of that responsibility. I do not take it lightly; nor should you.

Having said all of that, I did not want to write a book on the wonderful avenues by which women might minister to women in their local churches without also addressing the ministry of teaching. If you have a gift of teaching and you are feeling led to teach the women in your local church, I want to encourage you and guide you in that endeavor in the same way I have for all of the other areas I've included in these pages – by presenting you with a biblical example of a woman who taught in Scripture and by illustrating the particular character traits that make her a good example to follow. The lovely woman I will be highlighting for this ministry of teaching is Priscilla, or Prisca, as she was called by Paul.

One note before I move on, however. There is a lot of controversy within the Christian community about the place and role of female teachers within the church. It is indisputable that God bestows the gift of teaching on both men and women. The Bible is full of examples of this. The question arises, however, about whether women should teach just women and children or whether they should also teach men.

When discussing Deborah in the very first chapter of this book, I clearly defined biblical mandates on roles and order for men and women. However, since this is a book for women who desire to minister to women in their churches, I do not think it is necessary to present any case about whether or not women should also teach men. The teacher, as it will be defined in the following pages, is a teacher who teaches women. As we have done with the other women in this book, we will be examining Priscilla's character as a woman who taught the Word of God so that those of us who truly have a call to teach on our lives might find in her the type of woman who can teach with integrity in God's Kingdom.

YESTERDAY'S FOOTSTEPS

PRISCILLA — a Godly Woman and Teacher

Priscilla is mentioned a number of times in Scripture: Acts 18:2, 18, 26; Romans 16:3; 1 Corinthians 16:19; and 2 Timothy 4:19. However, she is never mentioned alone. Her name is always listed in conjunction with her husband, Aquila. Three times her name is listed first, and three times her husband's name is listed first. I will address the significance of this point later.

The point now is that she had a prominent place in Paul's ministry, and he obviously cared for her and her husband very deeply. He even took them with him on one of his missionary journeys to Ephesus, where Priscilla and Aquila started a church in their home.

Interestingly, this couple was in harmony and unison in their ministry of discipleship. The Bible doesn't say that Aquila went out and did the ministry while Priscilla stayed home and did the housework. They were a unit, both moving and working within the Christian community, both building the church and serving as companions to Paul.

Paul obviously loved this couple and had a special respect for Priscilla. That is evident not only in the fact that he sometimes addresses her first instead of her husband, which was absolutely opposite to the way those sorts of introductions were made in Jewish antiquity, but he also referred to her often as Prisca instead of Priscilla. Priscilla was considered the diminutive of Prisca, Prisca being the formal rendering of Priscilla. Paul's respect for Priscilla was evident in how he addressed her and how important he considered her to be within his ministry. Priscilla was certainly a woman to whom we can look for character traits necessary for a woman called to teach.

1. Priscilla ⁓ *a Strong and Industrious Woman*

When Paul first met Priscilla and her husband Aquila, he had just arrived in Corinth. Most likely, because Paul was so very intent on paying his own way, he was looking for work within the tent making trade. He found this couple who owned such a business. Their friendship developed quickly, so Paul stayed with them, most likely working the trade with them while he also spent much time teaching in the synagogues.

Tent making was no small, menial trade. It required great strength to lift and place large pieces of leather, waterproof them, and then carefully stitch the pieces together so the tent would remain waterproof. Priscilla was more than likely no stranger to hard work. Leather is heavy, especially during the waterproofing stage, and stitching those heavy pieces together in very tight stitches required great skill and strength. None of this might seem particularly notable were it not for what scholars have been able to surmise about her background.

Priscilla and Aquila were Jews who lived in Rome but were expelled by Claudius. However, ancient Roman inscriptions and legends give great prominence to Prisca's name, as well as to the name of her husband. Most likely, Priscilla and Aquila had been prominent Roman citizens before being expelled to Corinth. Though she most likely came from a family of some influence, Priscilla was no stranger to hard work. She worked alongside of her husband in their tent making trade, which for a short time also included

Paul, and then she joined her husband in the additionally hard work of running a home church in Ephesus. Truly an industrious and strong work ethic are character traits worth noting in this amazing woman of God.

2. Priscilla — *the Devoted Wife and Partner*

In every instance where Priscilla is mentioned in Scripture, she is paired with her husband. The two are one unit, one never named without the other. Yes, three times her name is mentioned first, and three times his is mentioned first, but more important than the order of the mentioning is the fact that they are always mentioned together. What a beautiful picture of harmony in these two God-honoring people. They labored together in their day-to-day trade, and they labored together in their kingdom work.

An article submitted to Bible Gateway beautifully sums up this relationship: "In the truest sense, Aquila and Priscilla were 'no more twain but one flesh,' and all that they covenanted to accomplish together from the hour of their marriage vows was realized as the result of the perfect unity of the spiritual, nature of purpose, and of aim. As twin stars, Aquila and Priscilla were 'bright with borrowed rays divine.' They moved in one orbit and were united in all their labors as well as in their love."[4]

Priscilla was obviously no glory-seeking prima donna who wanted the limelight for herself. The way all aspects of her life intertwined so beautifully with her husband's is a testimony to a woman with appropriate and God-honoring priorities. She may well have been the better teacher of the two. She may well have been more skilled in the tent-making business or more prosperous given her heritage, but none of that mattered to Priscilla. She understood God's priorities, placing God first, followed

---

[4] "Priscilla," *Bible Gateway, Zondervan,* 1988, https://www.biblegateway.com/resources/all-women-bible/Priscilla,03Feb.2016.

by her husband. Only in following her husband would there be any other ministry or vocation.

3. Priscilla — *the Hospitable Servant*

We read in Acts 18:3, after Paul's meeting Aquila and Priscilla, that *"...because he [Paul] was of the same trade he stayed with them and worked, for they were tentmakers by trade."*

Later, after traveling to Ephesus with Paul, Priscilla and Aquila again opened their home to others, both in hospitality and in teaching, to begin a church there. When she and Aquila heard Apollos speak, they invited him to their home so that they could share all they knew of the Gospel with him.

Again, though some records and inscriptions found might indicate a woman of high standing and intelligence, Priscilla was clearly a woman devoted to service and hospitality, especially as it served to promote the growth of the church. Beyond that, she was willing to serve in the ultimate capacity, even at the cost of her life. Paul wrote in Romans 16:3-4, *"Greet Prisca and Aquila, my fellow workers in Christ Jesus, who risked their necks for my life, to whom not only I give thanks but all the churches of the Gentiles give thanks as well."*

This couple was obviously willing to risk martyrdom for Paul's sake and for the sake of the Gospel. Paul's last mention of them was in his second letter to Timothy when the couple was back in Ephesus in AD 66 (2 Timothy 4:19). Tradition indicates that they ultimately did lay down their lives for the cause of Christ. July 8 is set aside in the record of martyrs of the Roman Church as a day to commemorate the occasion when the couple was led outside of the city walls and beheaded. Even in death, they were together, faithfully serving the church of Jesus Christ.

4. Priscilla — *a Woman Devoted to Scripture*

The Bible doesn't record the exact moment of Priscilla's or Aquila's conversion. We know that they were Jews expelled from Rome when Claudius sent them away and that they were living in Corinth when they met Paul for the first time. Although their shared skills of tent making initially brought them into contact with Paul, he afterward became friends with them and then moved in with them. Luke simply records in Acts 18:4, *"And he [Paul] reasoned in the synagogue every Sabbath, and tried to persuade the Jews and Greeks."*

It's safe to assume that Priscilla and her husband went to the synagogue too, since that was most likely the place where they heard Paul's testimony. Before they met Paul, they were already devout Jews, which meant that their devotion to the law was already in place.

Then in verses 24-27, we read that the two were in the synagogue again, this time as Christians, since this is where they first heard Apollos teach. They must have gone there regularly, likely teaching and sharing themselves. Otherwise, why would this very learned man so willingly come home with them and listen to what they had to say? Luke describes Apollos as "…an eloquent man, competent in the Scriptures" (Acts 18:24).

Priscilla and Aquila were apparently very devoted to the Word of God and to the Gospel of Jesus Christ, so much so that they were respected in the synagogue enough for someone like Apollos to be open to hearing from them. Consequently, this learned and eloquent speaker became a learned and eloquent believer who finally became an amazing advocate on behalf of Jesus as Lord and Savior.

5. Priscilla ⟶ *the Teacher*

As stated earlier, there is no doubt biblically that God gives the gift of teaching to both men and women. Timothy's grandmother, Lois, and his mother, Eunice, instructed Timothy in the way of Christ. (2 Timothy 1:15, 3:15) Deborah prophesied, which is a form of teaching, and Lydia led a church in her home. Additionally, Peter quoted the prophet Joel who wrote, *"And it shall come to pass afterward, that I will pour out my Spirit on all flesh; your sons and your daughters shall prophesy, your old men shall dream dreams, and your young men shall see visions."* (Joel 2:28). Consequently, there is little refutation to the truth that women both can and should teach.

In Acts 18:24-26, we see Priscilla and Aquila teaching Apollos the more fully revealed way of the gospel. Though many might put emphasis on the fact that once again Priscilla's name is mentioned first before her husband's, the real emphasis should be placed not on the order of the teachers but on the fact that Priscilla took part in instructing this already learned man in the doctrine of Christ.

As a matter of fact, the wording of verses 26-27 suggests in the original language that the couple took Apollos home with them and spent time with him, even bringing him to their church gathering. Verse 27 states, *"And when he* [Apollos] *wished to cross to Achaia, the brothers encouraged him and wrote to the disciples to welcome him."* (emphasis added) Who were these brothers if they were not church members? The Scripture indicates that Priscilla and Aquila spent time with Apollos, teaching him and leading him correctly.

God's Word is purposeful. Every word has meaning and purpose. It is inerrant. If that is the case, then we must surmise that Priscilla was involved in teaching along with her husband, or the Bible would have referred only to Aquila. Instead, both Priscilla and Aquila were given the enormous privilege and responsibility of correctly dividing God's Word so that Apollos would be effective in future kingdom work.

The question is not whether Priscilla, without her husband, should have been allowed to teach men, nor is that my point. The question is whether she, a woman, was allowed to teach God's Word, and the Bible clearly indicates here that she was. Priscilla was a mighty woman of God, submitted and devoted to her husband but also fully used in the office of teacher alongside of her husband.

Since Luke clearly describes this instance of a woman's teaching God's Word alongside of her husband, and since Paul clearly states in both Titus and 2 Timothy that women are to teach and train their children and other women in the church, it seems clear, according to God's Word, that a woman teaching other women in her local church is an established and God-honoring ministry. Likewise, if we are looking for an example of a woman with integrity and character to emulate in such a ministry, Priscilla is certainly an excellent candidate.

TODAY'S FOOTSTEPS

A Godly Woman and Teacher

The call to teach is, as stated above, a very serious call. But it is also a very blessed call. What a privilege to divide for others the very words of God! What an honor to be entrusted with the gift of proclaiming God's truths, His holiness, His justice, and His glorious path to salvation!

What an opportunity to be the avenue by which many will hear of God's greatness and move in a freedom made possible only by way of Jesus Christ! However, this tremendous gift comes at a cost, and great commitment and perseverance must accompany it. Necessary characteristics must be evident in a teacher of God's Word, and Priscilla's life more than measured up to those characteristics. How can her integrity and God-honoring lifestyle translate into practical applications for women considering this very important ministry?

1. No Laziness Allowed!

A great deal of work is involved in teaching, and not all of that work is in preparation. However, beyond the act of teaching and necessary preparation, a woman truly called to this type of ministry must display a work ethic that is manifested in all of her life. Priscilla worked hard beside her husband in their family trade, exhibiting a work ethic that qualified her to be teacher of God's Word.

A teacher should first display a sense of excellence in all that she does. Being a woman of excellence is a quality that should be present in all forms of ministry, but for the woman who presumes to present God's Word in applicable ways to the women in her church, being a woman of excellence is non-negotiable. Do you strive for the best in all that you do? Are you satisfied with a house half-cleaned, a lesson partially completed, a family marginally taken care of? Although these questions may seem at first glance to have nothing whatsoever to do with teaching, one will be able to ascertain the standards she lives by in her own life by answering these questions. The standard we accept in managing our household will reflect the standard by which we will divide God's Word.

A strong work ethic is paramount in the life of a teacher because teaching takes much study, preparation, and time. There are no shortcuts. Reading, meditating, praying, studying, writing, practicing, memorizing – all of these are commonly practiced by any good teacher. However, those things cannot take priority over her first priority within God's kingdom, and that is taking care of her household. Whether married with children still at home, widowed, single, or living in the empty nest stage of life, women have been given the primary responsibility and precious job of taking care of the home. This is not a demeaning position. It is extraordinarily important to God – so important that He created us and uniquely equipped us to perform it. Teaching does not supersede this job, but how we complete this managerial position will indicate whether or not we are truly fit to be a teacher.

Again, I know this isn't a popular concept in today's 21st century society. But if a woman is unable or unwilling to take care of the people and places within her home, how can she be trusted to rightly divide God's word for women with the same responsibilities? Properly caring for your family is an immovable standard, and like Priscilla, teachers in the church simply have to live by it.

2. She is Devoted to Her Spouse and Family

The strong work ethic leads wonderfully into the second character trait in which Priscilla excels: devotion to her family. So many women have bought into what mainstream society has been selling in terms of self-actualization and self-concern. Today's woman wants a career, and her family is on the back burner. If she is in a position where she gets to stay at home with her children, she often feels guilty, as if she isn't fulfilling all that she can be.

Husbands are seen as more of a liability and a stumbling block than an opportunity to mirror our eternal marriage to Jesus Christ. The modern woman would never consider sharing the limelight with her husband, much less feel satisfied with being known as a unit instead of as an independent woman.

Within the framework of the church, a woman who feels called to teach the women in her church must stand against all that the world would teach about womanhood and what that looks like. She should be so consumed with God and His Word that society and its preferences are of no consequence to her calling. She stands tall with her husband or with her children or with the leadership in her church. If she doesn't have a husband or children at home, her disposition must still be one that advocates that kind of humble view on kingdom standing.

A woman who teaches in the church must not be centered on self. She must be centered on God and what He has mandated for her life. Notoriety, wealth, position, and reputation are of no concern to her, and when that is the case, she can stand boldly and confidently as a partner with her husband. She can stand with her children as their mother. Only then can she represent the holy avenues of the Bible with integrity and God-centeredness.

3. She has a Servant Mindset

For a number of years, I was the women's ministry director at a local church, and I also taught the women's Bible study. After one lesson, a few of us were busy cleaning up the coffee and snacks when a woman who attended came to me to say that she felt the call to teach. I smiled and nodded, waiting for her to continue. Her next words confirmed for me that she definitely was not called to this ministry.

"You see," she began, "I'm not called to put out the chairs or make coffee or clean up." She was motioning toward the wonderful women doing just those things around her. "I'm called to teach."

I looked her right in the eyes as I continued to clean the table we were sitting at and said, "I'm sorry, but if you're not called to serve, you are certainly not called to teach."

She walked away, and I never saw her again.

The notion that one would be called to stand up and teach a message about a God who clearly told us to serve one another above all else while not serving is quite frankly ludicrous. No teacher is exempt from service. Chair stacking, coffee making, table setting, set up, and clean up are all jobs a teacher should be both willing to do and doing. If you are feeling as if God is leading you to teach a Bible study or anything else in your church, be prepared to make some coffee. Be prepared to stack a few chairs or wash a few dishes. Not one of those women will be willing to listen to someone speak to them about a doctrine of service when that someone won't personally demonstrate service herself.

4. She is All About the Word

Indulge me for a moment in another example. While leading the women's ministry in the local church I mentioned before, I had many women at different times come to me to say they felt called to teach. Generally, they were looking for me to give them an opportunity to do so with our ladies. Of course, I was never against giving such opportunities and tried to work it in as often as possible. However, over the years, I began to develop a sort of litmus test for when a woman was really being called to teach or when she was instead being called to stand on stage with a microphone. My number one litmus test was watching the devotion to study or the lack thereof in these women.

A certain woman who used to help set things up and do a little administrative work for me was one of the many women who approached me with a desire to teach. I let her do a small testimony, and though she was nervous and a little tentative, what I noticed most was her lack of biblical preparation. Then I began to observe more.

Our women's ministry Bible studies included a large gathering, where the message was brought, and then the ladies broke up into small groups to discuss the study questions for that week. I began to notice that this particular woman, who helped divide women into groups, never attended one. She would sit in the back and "oversee" the groups. I then also began to notice that she didn't do the study herself. Her pages were blank.

I asked her questions about the readings, and it became apparent that she wasn't reading the books. Eventually I confronted her about her desire to teach with no accompanying desire for the Word. It didn't go well. She became convinced that I was simply trying to "keep her down" or "not utilize her to her fullest potential."

It truly was sad, but what was most sad about that situation is how common it is. The notion of teaching – standing in the center of a stage with a microphone in hand and all eyes trained on you – is an appealing notion to many, but for all the wrong reasons. The desire to teach absolutely must be born from a desire for God's Word. When you see the beauty contained within it and the freedom it brings, the desire to teach becomes more of a desire to share the wonderful things you've learned yourself. Your need to teach on stage isn't a need for the stage at all. Your need is to show how amazing God is and to tell as many women as you can, in whatever means available to you, the truths of the Lord. That's the call to teach. It's a call that begins first with a clear and distinct love of Scripture. It's a call that originates in devotion to study and prayer and meditation. The actual teaching part of it is just an outpouring of the love for what you've learned from God about God.

That's what obviously drove Priscilla, and this must be what drives you if indeed you are called to this very wonderful ministry.

5. She has the Gift of Teaching

Finally, let me offer a very practical application. If one is really called to minister to women in her church by means of teaching, she must be able to perform the act of teaching. In other words, you have to be able to teach. Of course, one can be trained in the nuances of the teaching craft. I was an educator in the public school system for eighteen years before going into ministry. My master's degree is in the art of teaching. I definitely understand that a person can be taught to teach. However, that's not necessarily what I am referring to here.

I'm referring to the gift of teaching, that God-given ability to share a story, make a point, engage an audience, remain sincere, be relatable, and just plain be able to keep someone's attention for longer than thirty seconds. The question is not so much, "Can you teach?" The question is more like, "Can you share the intricacies of God's truths to a group of people in a way that they both understand and can apply?" In other words, "Can you talk to them about God?"

Answering a question like this one requires serious introspection, and it requires you to be honest with yourself. If you really are called into this area of ministry, you absolutely will be able to answer in the affirmative, even if you realize that you might need some help. That's okay. We all do! However, it is of the utmost importance that you know for sure that teaching is something you are gifted to do, even if you're not quite sure of exactly how to do it. God will work with your weaknesses.

The call to teach is so serious. I can't stress that point enough, but I also don't want to dissuade anyone who is truly feeling that this is the way

God is calling them to minister to the women in their local church. If He is calling you, He will equip you. Just be sure the call is from Him, not you.

If I'm a Priscilla, where Do I Start?

Teaching about God's Word and how it applies to the lives of women is an amazing way to minister to the women in your church. It's an honor and a privilege, but it's hard work, and it takes serious commitment. It's not for everyone, but it is definitely for some. I want to personally encourage any of you who have read through this chapter and come to the conclusion that this ministry is one you would like to explore as the possible new thing God wants to do through you. I do have a few practical suggestions as to where to begin. I pray they are a help to you.

- Stop, drop to your knees, and pray like you've never prayed before. Teaching is not only serious in terms of what you do, but the minute you take up this very sacred mantle, you shift into a position in God's eyes where your accountability has just increased exponentially. The Lord will hold you responsible for every word you utter using that gift, so please pray like your life depends on it. In many ways, it does.

- No matter where you are in the seasons of your life, become a student of God's Word. Make sure to be in Bible studies as often as you can. Be in church, seated and ready to receive from the pulpit every single weekend, mid-week, and whenever the doors are open and you can be there. Be attentive. Take notes. Ask questions. Then study, study, study.

Every opportunity you have, study some more. You cannot represent God's Word if you aren't fully prepared.

- Listen to/watch other teachers. Take note of the simple things they do: how they move around the platform, what format their lessons take, or when and how they use illustrations. You can learn a lot by listening to and watching other experienced and seasoned teachers.

- If possible, take a training class on how to develop lessons and how to study your Bible effectively. All of these tools will come in handy as you prepare your own messages.

- Make an appointment with your pastor and talk to him about the possibility of teaching. He is your shepherd, and you absolutely must not operate out from under the covering of the leadership in your church. Be open and honest with him but also be willing to hear what he has to say. Your church may not have many opportunities for a woman to teach women at this point. If not, then continue to hone the skill of teaching until it does. I can promise you that if God has called you to this particular ministry, the opportunity will arise, but it will arise in God's proper order and under your pastor's leadership. Don't be discouraged if your pastor isn't on the exact same page with you yet. If you both agree to be open to God's leading, then you are on the same page.

- If your pastor is in agreement with you about teaching something right away, then ask for suggestions on material. Make sure that whatever you choose is in line with your church's doctrine and get prior approval before moving ahead with any topic. Each church will have its own procedure, so be sure to follow whatever that is.

- More than anything else, either while you are teaching or while you are waiting until the time is right to begin teaching, find somewhere to serve in your church. Believe me, no one will want to sit under your instruction if they haven't first seen you serving their interests and needs in other ways. You are building trust, and you are demonstrating Jesus in doing so. Besides, this is your church family. Be a part of it!

Please know that my intention in the last several pages has not been to discourage you or scare you away from the ministry of teaching. I simply desire to be honest and forthright, sharing with you not only what I've gleaned over the years through study of God's Word but also the practical applications I've seen played out in my own life as a minister.

God bless you as you move forward from here. My prayer for you is Paul's declaration to the church in Rome in Romans 10:14-15, *"But how are they to call on him whom they have not believed? And how are they to believe in him of whom they have never heard? And how are they to hear without someone preaching? And how are they to preach unless they are sent? As it is written, 'How beautiful are the feet of those who preach the good news!'"*

Concluding Thoughts

I absolutely love being a woman! I love the unique aspects of womanhood and the distinct and different way God created us. I love talking to women and sharing life's struggles and victories together. And I love watching women fulfill their particular gifts within the church.

What I don't love is observing women who are so lonely and discontent in their lives and in their churches that it is discontentment and loneliness that display themselves in every facet of their lives. They come to church on Sunday morning, say the obligatory hello to the people they see, sit in the pew and sing "Amazing Grace" at the top of their lungs, listen to the message and maybe even take a few notes here and there, and then they go home. They aren't involved in the church in any capacity, besides maybe passing out a bulletin every once in a while or taking their turn in the nursery. They live fully separated from their church family.

My sisters, this should not be! Our church is our family, and in that family are so many women who need you. They need you in some capacity, and you need them. You need to be ministered to by them, and you need to minister to them. I pray that you have read this book – really read it – and I pray that you have been pricked in your heart about ministry in your church, ministry specifically from women to women. I cannot stress enough that if you aren't doing something to minister to the women who are in your eternal family, then you are missing out on one of the greatest joys this life has to offer as you sojourn here.

Take a chance. Find a place to be knit to like-minded beings – the women in your local church body! Step into the beautiful sandals that have been laid out before you. Only joy and community will be the result.

May the Lord bless you and keep you, and may his grace shine down upon you. Amen.

lovetruthlive

WITH DEB WATERBURY

Teaching that the love of Christ
and the Truth of Scripture lead
to life-changing freedom

*"By this all people will
know that you are my
disciples, if you have
love for one another."*
– John 13:35

debwaterbury.com

lovetruthlive
WITH DEB WATERBURY

PAINTED WINDOW TRILOGY:
Painted Window, Threads and White Zephyr

Follow Elizabeth Percy's allegorical
journey into discovering the love
that transforms all of our lives –
the love of Jesus, our Bridegroom.

James on the Mount

A study of the book of James as it relates
to the Sermon on the Mount.

DAILY DEVOTIONAL SERIES:

Bible devotional studies, verse by verse.

- *Galatians* (3 month devotional)
- *Ephesians* (3 month devotional)
- *Philippians* (3 month devotional)

WOMEN'S MINISTRY STUDIES:

6 Pairs of Sandals
Yesterday's Footsteps and Today's
Women's Ministry

ADDITIONAL RESOURCES AT

www.debwaterbury.com

Dr. Deb Waterbury
also offers:
Windows of the Heart Podcast Teachings
(also available through iTunes)
and
Voices of Love Blogs

Visit us on Facebook, Twitter, Instagram,
LinkedIn, Pinterest and YouTube

Note:
*Dr. Deb Waterbury continues to expand
her resource catalogue, so please log onto
her website for the most recent additions.*

Made in the USA
Monee, IL
05 November 2020